All Tomorrow's Cultures

ALL TOMORROW'S CULTURES

Anthropological Engagements with the Future

Samuel Gerald Collins

berghahn

NEW YORK · OXFORD

www.berghahnbooks.com

First edition published in 2008 by

Berghahn Books
www.berghahnbooks.com

© 2008, 2021 Samuel Gerald Collins
Revised Edition published in 2021.

Library of Congress Cataloging-in-Publication Data

Collins, Samuel Gerald.
   All tomorrow's cultures : anthropological engagements with the future / Samuel Gerald Collins. — 1st ed.
      p.   cm.
   Includes bibliographical references and index.
   ISBN-13: 978-1-84545-408-1 (hardback : alk. paper)
   1. Anthropology—Philosophy. 2. Future in popular culture. I. Title.
GN33.C64 2007
301.01—dc22

                                                    2007015622

British Library Cataloguing in Publication Data

A catalogue record for this book is available from the British Library

Printed in the United States on acid-free paper

ISBN 978-1-80073-076-2 hardback
ISBN 978-1-80073-078-6 paperback
ISBN 978-1-80073-077-9 ebook

To my wife, children, and their surprising futures.

Contents

❦

List of Figures

Preface to the Revised Edition
Anthropology of the Future /
The Future of Anthropology / Anthropological Futures

When the first edition of this book was published in 2008, the future was
not often recognized as an object of anthropological inquiry. The operative
word here is "recognized," since, as the following chapters document, anthropologists have long been concerned with the future and the speculative.
It's just that anthropologists were not accustomed to thinking of themselves
as engaging in future work. But, even then, much of anthropology involved
the future. In a thoughtful review essay of recent future work in anthropology, Valentine and Hassoun reflect on the amnesia of the field to its own
futural orientations: "Yet, a review of anthropological literature published
since the end of the Cold War tells a different story: that futurity has become a dominant, even primary, temporality in the discipline as an analytic
frame, ethnographic project, methodological concern, and—significantly—
affective mode" (Valentine and Hassoun 2019: 244). This seems obvious if
we consider the postwar development of the field. In applied or public anthropology, the focus is continuously on the future—through developmental
discourse, through policy interventions. If we chronicle hopes, dreams, and
fears of people, then we are concerned with the future (Bryant and Knight
2019). And if we attempt to address racism, white supremacy, and police
brutality through our anthropology, then we are also engaging in future
work. Here "the future" is just part of human life, and our understanding of
the future is, similarly, embedded in our own conditions as humans at the
intersection of time, place, and identity.

If future-work in anthropology was mostly unacknowledged when the
first edition came out, the last decade has seen a sharp growth in explicit engagements with future temporalities. We can even pinpoint this moment. If
we examine meetings hosted by the American Anthropological Association
and the European Association of Social Anthropologists (among others), we

see a dramatic increase in future- and science-fiction-oriented panels from 2011. At the American Anthropological Association, the high point was undoubtedly the 2017 meetings, when there was an unprecedented number of papers and panels exploring the contours of futures in the contexts of anthropological method and theory with the ultimate goal of working to change the present. This is clearly anthropology's anticipatory moment, and we see scholars from multiple subdisciplines (STS, environmental anthropology, urban anthropology, etc.) exploring what futures might be evoked in the space of anthropological intervention. The methods and potentials of this are being shaped right now, and a renewed orientation toward future-work (broadly) is forming.

Of course, there's not a consensus, and this does not represent the coalescence of a stable paradigm. This can be seen in my analysis of the 2019 AAA/CASCA conference (held in Vancouver). The graphs below utilize "Infranodus" (a semantic network mapping website) to generate a semantic map showing co-occurrences of terms in session abstracts linked to the keyword "future." The dots (or nodes) represent words (or lemmas that might

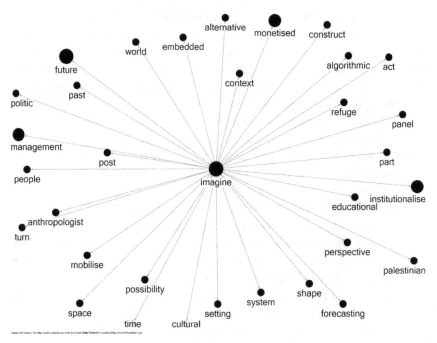

Figure 0.1. The connections between "imagine" and other terms in a network formed from future-oriented abstracts for the 2019 American Anthropological Association Annual / Canadian Anthropology Society Meeting in Vancouver. Created by the author.

represent several variations), and the lines between them other words that co-occur in sentences.

The first shows the terms linked to "future" and "imagine." The network formed by "imagine" and "future" sketches a path toward programmatic changes that intervene in this political moment to open up possibilities—even utopian possibilities. On the other hand, there are a number of other terms—"institutionalize," "management," "monetized"—that suggest the limits to imagination in the form of capitalism and institutional practice.

This is similar in the second graph, this time highlighting "future" and "climate." The focus on climate, on the Anthropocene, and on environmental catastrophe seems to preclude utopian speculation. Here, anthropologists are caught in the seeming inevitability of environmental collapse, although note that lemmas like "change" and "adaptation" offer something more like a Donna Haraway "staying with the trouble" approach to disaster (Haraway 2016).

The third graph looks to lemmas connected to "future" and "alternative." With connections to "emerging," "utopian," "world" and "space," "alternative" charts a course for more speculative futures. These futures also

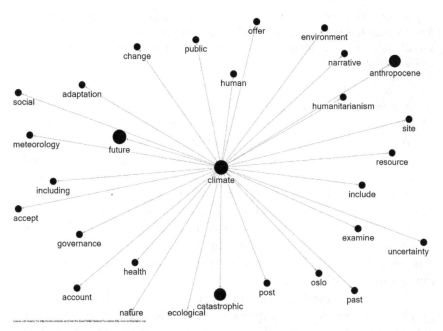

Figure 0.2. The connections between "climate" and other terms in a network formed from future-oriented abstracts for the 2019 American Anthropological Association Annual / Canadian Anthropology Society Meeting in Vancouver. Created by the author.

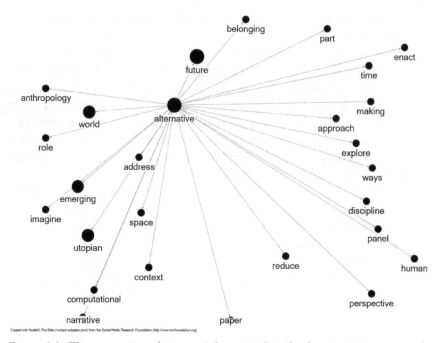

Figure 0.3. The connections between "alternative" and other terms in a network formed from future-oriented abstracts for the 2019 American Anthropological Association Annual / Canadian Anthropology Society Meeting in Vancouver. Created by the author.

seem to include anthropology as well, as a discipline still grappling for its identity amid its continued embeddedness in colonialism and empire.

Across climate change, the necessity for alternatives, and evocation of utopia, the future work evolving in anthropology engages multiple levels, including: (1) "the future" as something articulated, feared, and longed-for by anthropology's informants; (2) "the future" as an object of analysis and critique through an examination of popular culture, philosophy, and literature; and (3) the future as a place where anthropologists themselves might intervene and plot alternatives. Like our informants and collaborators, anthropologists, too, negotiate multiple futures in our lives and research (Bryant and Knight 2019).

Conference papers are, of course, harbingers of articles and monographs. Published work in anthropology has followed, and similar themes are evident in the monographs anthropologists have produced. First, following on the landmark 2004 ethnography from Hirokazu Miyazaki on Fijian land reform, anthropologists have examined hopes and fears for the future in numerous ways, underscoring both the importance of the future and ways those future orientations impinge upon present action (Miyazaki 2004).

Second, more and more anthropologists have taken "the future" (however conceived) as their research object. Here (as perhaps, everywhere) the anthropological object is emergent—like Morton's "hyper-objects," the sites where anthropologists study are temporal phenomena, sites where future actualizations are not necessarily implicit in the present. As in Abbott's 1884 "Flatland," the future exists in the present in an impoverished form—its complexity is hidden from us. Small wonder that simplistic, linear prognostications are what pass in the popular presses as "futurology." Anthropologists work against the tendency to ascribe contemporary inequalities to the future, to project a "path dependency" on racial or gendered inequality into what we believe the world will become. What this means, though, varies by anthropologist and research. It includes, variously, anthropologists like Lisa Messeri, whose research in *Placing Outer Space* considers the emergent construction of exoplanets—itself a subdiscipline deeply implicated in prognosticating futures of human exploration (Messeri 2016). Here, she joins a number of other space researchers who consider the ways present contours of space planning and exploration work toward the construction of human futures. Similarly, Valerie Olson's *Into the Extreme* examines the real and simulated movements of people through extreme environments, environments that rehearse our extraplanetary futures (Olson 2018). Alice Gorman's work on "space junk" likewise builds an archaeology of the suborbital detritus that clouds the exosphere and thermosphere of our planet, but she also imagines encountering the Earth and the solar system from without, and what this might tell us about human futures. As she ends her autobiographical *Dr. Space Junk vs. the Universe*,

> Outside Earth, we may finally see what the characteristics of human nature really are. Which ones persist will be those we can't escape by reason of our biology and evolutionary history. They will be the basis of human evolution as a multigravity species" (Gorman 2019: 273)

Finally, anthropologists have begun to utilize tropic invocations of the future in their ethnographic work, eschewing more conventional representations for "more radical future possibilities that may confound those of prediction and forecasting" (Salazar et al. 2017: 12). These interventions proceed from not only a critique of anthropology's objects but also from a critique of the ways that the "ethnographic real" presupposes temporal linearity, one that slots the cultural other into the past while naturalizing Western hegemony into an impoverished future. Between work like Escobar's *Designs for the Pluriverse*, Biehl and Locke's *Unfinished*, and Pandian's *A Possible*

Anthropology, anthropologists have begun to describe an anthropology that supports the establishment of alternative futures (Escobar 2017; Biehl and Locke 2017; Pandian 2020).

But what form might that anthropology take? As Wolf-Meyer asks, "What sources might there be for rethinking the future? for dislodging the futures that we have been given and to think something anew? for rethinking the past that has gotten us to this point? Articulating futures—imagining them and bringing them into being—is an active process, and rather than a posture of resignation, theory for the world to come needs to instill radical curiosity" (Wolf-Meyer 2019). The old ethnographic forms may not prove adequate. Or, rather, "writing culture" as we've come to know and practice it may prove, ultimately, a logocentric exercise that works to buttress Western, white hegemony at the expense of genuine difference. Here, we see people experimenting with form as well, through multimodal anthropology, through performance, or through adopting other, nontextual platforms. Consider work like Elizabeth Chin's and Danya Glabau's "Wakanda University" installations/performances at American Anthropological Association meetings. Utilizing multiple media, Chin and Glabau have both critiqued the embeddedness of anthropology in structures of colonial domination while still gesturing to emancipatory directions (Chin and Galbau 2019). This is where anthropology and science fiction meet, but their intersection serves to interrogate what we mean by both.

These are "speculative ethnographies," defined by Oman-Reagan as "any creative engagement with possible futures crafted using imaginative anthropological approaches toward the aim of building just and ethical relations across spatial and temporal scales (Oman-Reagan 2018). And they are the heir to anthropology's future work (Chin and Glabau 2019). In a way, I hope that these recent experiments don't coalesce into a canonical approach to futures. The multidirectionality of these evocations is the best feature of this round of future-oriented research: urban, multispecies, reproductive technologies, SF, dystopia, journalism, government policy. Here the future is multiple, and my instinct would be to contribute to open futures through our anthropologies rather than joining with, say, the dismal science to close off differences through model-driven prognostications.

And this is really what this monograph is about: revisiting past entanglements with the future in order to help ensure that our future will not be a mere recapitulation of the past. But it is also about anthropology's future. Over the past few years of rising fascism, white supremacist violence, and reactionary politics, it has become clear where anthropology has facilitated this authoritarian nightmare. A turn to the future is, in this respect, a recuperative strategy for a discipline's guilty past. Finally, it is an argument for a properly utopian imagination and, correspondingly, against the knee-jerk dystopian "realism." Yes—we can characterize the present moment as "dystopian" in several ways. Certainly, revanchist white supremacy, authoritarian governments, fascism on the rise, pandemics, and school violence all have the trappings of fairly run-of-the-mill dystopian fare. But we're not living in dystopia. Instead, as China Mieville wrote, "We live in a utopia, it just isn't ours" (Mieville 2018). "Dystopia" has that sense of accident, of things being taken too far: the robots win, there's too much surveillance, soylent green is people, etc. But things today work exactly as they were designed to "work." Flagrantly unequal policies, structural racism, environmental ruin: these are deliberate choices that have brought immeasurable wealth and power to a few people while disenfranchising most people, and especially those people that have most often been the subjects for anthropological research. And the result is a utopia for racists and fascists who can bask in the ruddy horror of the fear and abjection that they have helped create.

At the heart of this book is the realization that anthropology has been sometimes critical of this utopia, sometimes complicit in it, but that the way forward must be to create alternatives to the brutal utopias around us. We have a moral injunction not only to interrogate power and inequality today but also to work toward societies that are better than they are now. The message of this book is that this is not a new mission for anthropology—just one that needs a renewed emphasis. Indeed, the final chapter in this book again circles back to nineteenth-century beginnings for inspiration we might take. But also for a critical focus. More than ever before, anthropology needs to interrogate its role vis-à-vis the legitimation of the status quo and the naturalization of capitalism's inequalities. If future work in anthropology merely reproduces an etiolated present, then it is just a propaganda mouthpiece.

Acknowledgments

Parts of the Introduction and Chapter 5 have been previously published as "Sail On! Sail On!: Anthropology, Science Fiction and the Enticing Future" (2003). *Science Fiction Studies* 30(2): 180–198; Chapter 3 has been previously published as "'Scientifically Valid and Artistically True': Chad Oliver, Anthropology and Anthropological Science Fiction." (2004). *Science Fiction Studies* 31(2): 243–263. The author would like to thank of editors of Science Fiction Studies for permission to reprint those essays here.

Chapter 6 has been previously published as "Anthropology, Emergence and the Shock of the Foregone" (2007). *After Culture* 1(1). The author would like to thank the editor of *After Culture* for permission to reprint the essay here.

Much of the research for this book has been supported by various Towson University Faculty Development grants, for which the author is eternally grateful.

Additional thanks go to Reed Riner, Hal Hall and Matthew Wolf-Meyer, who have all been generous with their time and their ideas.

Introduction

Tomorrow's Cultures Today?

Were it not for its blatant, reactionary conservatism, anthropologists might have been excited by Samuel Huntington's 1993 prophecy that "the great divisions among humankind and the dominating source of conflict will be cultural" (Huntington 1993: 22). Finally, an admonition of the salience of culture! Of course, that's not quite what Huntington meant, and anthropologists, along with a host of other critics, have picked apart the desultory confusion of civilization, religion, language, race and politics that make up the "units" of Huntington's paean to Arnold Toynbee (Besteman and Gusterson 2005; Hannerz 2003; Palumbo-Liu 2002; Said 2001; Tuastad 2003). The absurd stereotyping that pits "Islamic," "Buddhist," and "Confucian" civilizations against the "West" alternates between the moronic and the Machiavellian; it is no mistake that Huntington's work has become a master text in the twenty-first century drive toward US global hegemony. Perhaps because of the wealth of pernicious error, however, few critics have examined the temporal confusions in Huntington's discourse. Each "civilization" seems to be stuck in a given timeline: for example, the "West" with modernity and capitalism (eighteenth century), China with "Confucianism" (Han Dynasty, 141 BCE), "Arabs" with Islam (seventh century CE). Each of these "civilizations" follows the dictates of its civilizational imperative, a wind-up cultural discord that "clashes" in the present. The future is said to depend on whether or not these cultural pasts will become the future, whether or not "non-Western countries" will "join" the "West" (the instinct to bracket everything here is difficult to resist). But are we talking about the present or the past? Join modernity (usually attributed to the eighteenth century)? This is most evident in Huntington's discussion of "torn" countries, where the weird, cultural time warps are more evident. Russia is characterized not only as belonging to the "modern" (via Marxism), but also to the "Slavic-Orthodox" (seventh century CE with the development of Russian?):

> A Western democrat could carry on an intellectual debate with a Soviet Marxist. It would be virtually impossible for him to do that with a Russian traditionalist. If, as Russians stop behaving like Marxists, they reject liberal democracy and begin behaving like Russians but not like Westerners, the relations between Russia and the West could again become distant and conflictual. (1993: 44–45)

What's interesting here is not only the now-familiar tactic of placing other peoples in the past of the West (that is, tradition versus modernity), but also in the strange multiplication of timelines—each "civilization" is characterized by a sort of distinct timespace aligning through shared, cultural temporalities (Huntington's "kin-country" syndrome). Cocooned in their (other) temporalities, civilizations, in a way vaguely reminiscent of time travel episodes on *Star Trek: The Next Generation,* are unable to communicate with one another. The "West" seems just as much a slave to the past as anyone else (albeit on a different timeline) and the future for Huntington means not a convergence of timelines, but rather their multiplication in the frisson of the "clash." The future of culture, then, is always already the return to the past.

This has long been the paradox of culture, where the present collapses onto the past on its way to a future that can only be the recapitulation of what came before. It is, for example, at the heart of Matthew Arnold's 1869 prescriptions for cultural progress, where we "progress" toward perfection guided by, as Arnold wrote, "the best which has been thought and said in the world," that is, a Janus-faced adulation of past "civilization" en route to a future illuminated in the penumbra of the past. "Progress" here appears as curiously retrograde: forward, yet backward; different than today, yet ultimately dependent upon its consonance with yesterday.

And it is exactly the case with globalization today, which combines a faith and belief in perpetual change (Schumpeterian creative destruction) with an abyssal vision of repetition and stasis, an Elidean myth of the eternal return for advanced capitalism where we "progress" to a state of free market nature that is supposed to have always existed beneath a patina of State planning.

Consider a recent myth, the novel *Cosmopolis* (2003) by Don DeLillo, which chronicles the slow fall of a New Economy wunderkind Eric Packer as he travels down forty-seventh street in midtown Manhattan to get a haircut. True to myth, it is a curiously haunting, contradictory novel, which, nevertheless, tells us a great deal about the eerie similarities to the world we ascribe to the West's imagined others and the world we think we live in.

In *Cosmopolis,* time is defined by perpetual, vertiginous change, with every event, invention, or fad cresting and disappearing in increasingly accelerated sinusoid distributions. It is life in the shadow of Moore's Law (chip density doubles every eighteen months)—unending "creative destruction."[1] In this accelerated world, things become obsolete almost as soon as they are introduced:

> He took out his hand organizer and poked a note to himself about the word sky-scraper. No recent structure ought to bear this word. It belonged to the olden soul of awe, to the narrowed towers that were a narrative long before he was born.
>
> The hand device itself was an object whose original culture had just about disappeared. He knew he'd have to junk it. (9)

This is accelerating "creative destruction"—first the skyscraper then, a heart-beat later, the PDA upon which the demise of the skyscraper has been writ-ten. In *Cosmopolis,* "all that is solid melts into air" gives way to something even more ephemeral—one airy mass blowing into the next, with nothing ever solidifying at all. Eric's slow trip to his eventual demise traces the ephemerality of all culture and social life in the age of globalization where nothing will really matter (or literally *be* matter) for long.

In the end, even time itself proves curiously outré, melting under the glare of white-hot advanced capitalism. Eventually, "future," "present," and "past" all seem like media effects, as when Eric's own CCTV cameras broad-cast his own future:

> His own image caught his eye, live on the oval screen beneath the spycam. Some seconds passed. He saw himself recoil in shock. More time passed. He felt suspended, waiting. Then there was a detonation, loud and deep, near enough to consume all the information around him. He recoiled in shock. Everyone did. (93)

In the speed-up of advanced capitalism that critics like Paul Virilio decry (but also, perhaps, celebrate), media represent the future to us rather than the present or past. "Progress" becomes so ubiquitous that the shadowy world of "non-progress" is utterly occulted in its blinding glare. The speed of information and the rate of advance and obsolescence have increased to the point of media singularity. This is, after all, one of the motors of advanced capitalism—creating, for example, a state of perpetual expectation for the next generation of information technologies, the frantic sense of a gap be-tween what one owns and the more advanced products that one should be buying. In advanced capitalism, we are urged to buy the future.

But does this mean that change accelerates? There are two ways, after all, to look at this: a state of perpetual change is the same as perpetual stasis.

Ubiquitous acceleration is the same as standing still. Fukuyama's "end of history" suggests the extent to which time is discounted in the global age.[2]

When Eric sees his own future, it may not be a sign of proleptic speed-up but rather an indication that the future itself has ceased to be meaningful. That is, "the future" has become the preferred modality for living in the present and can be said to no longer exist "in front" of us at all; in the world of consumption, it actually seems to exist *behind* us, as products we do not yet own. Instead of a future characterized by the brachiating of new possibilities and unforeseen occurrences, we get the rapid, linear succession of "new" products that are endless iterations of consumer desire succeeding one another like cards on a blackjack table. This is one of the most malefi-cent effects of globalization: the attenuation of alternatives to market-driven teleologies. We don't need to speculate on what the future may bring when the answer is on the next page of the catalog. Thinking outside of these narrow futures has passed from being heretical (in the Cold War) to being ridiculous—the subject of fantasy rather than speculation.

This has been sorely evident in the "culture wars," largely a conservative invention that pits its "values" and "civilization"-based protagonists against parodic representations of intellectuals propounding what looks to be, in fact, a very mild multiculturalism. As one of the conservative demagogues, Lee Harris (2004: 218), instructs his straw-men interlocutors:

> Intellectuals in America, Europe, and elsewhere must abandon the pursuit of abstract utopias and fantasy ideologies and return to the real world. They must undertake a critique of their own inherent distorted points of view, in order to comprehend the visceral and emotional dynamic at the foundation of all human cultures and their history. They must cease to attack those codes of honor that the modern West has inherited from its various traditions, political, cultural, and religious. They must not permit the culture war within the West to degenerate, as it threatens to do, into a civil war.

True to the McCarthy-esque spirit, Harris calls for a sinister reeducation in order to safeguard the security of the nation. And, again similar to the McCarthy era, the "enemies" with whom he struggles are more or less imag-inary. The "tenured radicals" making the blacklist of GOP-funded think tanks are not, after all, advocating utopian communes; for the most part, what drives conservatives into apoplectic rages are the rather mild admoni-tions that the government should make good on its own vague multicultur-alism and acknowledge the many, structural inequalities that bedevil the supposedly raceless and classless society in the US. In contrast to Harris's stentorian ultimatums, the scholarship of, say, Michael Bérubé impresses with its comparatively benign calls for tolerance. See, for example, David

Horowitz's *The Professors: The Most 101 Dangerous Academics in America* where people who would never have been fingered as "radicals" in the 1960s and 1970s are excoriated as the enemies of liberal democracy, including Elizabeth Brumfiel, an archaeologist and ethnohistorian whose research on class and gender dynamics in Mesoamerica and Aztec civilization does not exactly constitute a clarion call for the revolution (cf. Brumfiel and Fox 1996).

What this all shows is that conservatives have already limited debate to a set of hypostatized binarisms that facilitate their facile observations and broad stereotypes: West and non-West, meritocracy and affirmative action. In these terms, debate, such as it is, is largely over before it has even begun. That is, what are missing in these "culture wars" are actual alternatives: As Jameson (1991: 281) complains, "The surrender to various forms of market ideology—on the *Left*, I mean, not to mention everyone else—has been imperceptible but alarmingly universal. Everyone is now willing to mumble, as though it were an inconsequential concession in passing to public opinion and current received wisdom (or shared communicational presuppositions), that no society can function efficiently without the market, and that planning is obviously impossible."

Accompanying the economic realism that informs this universal acceptance of the "market" has been a similar iron consensus coalescing around the idea of culture. The notion of a banal homogenization of culture is treated as more or less axiomatic in the global age. The political spectrum devolves around whether the opening of a T.G.I. Fridays in Ankara should be celebrated or decried. Other cultures are to be preserved (literally, in many cases, placed in a preserve) as part of vague patrimony for the world, but no one's pinning their hopes on systems of generalized reciprocity for the twenty-first century. Indeed, the degree to which the "culture wars" present a consensus about what exactly "culture" is and what it will be is what I find most disturbing. Like Eric stuck in traffic in DeLillo's novel, culture in the age of globalization is on its way to nowhere; the future will be shelling out the same hamburgers.

So, if the future for the Ancient Greeks exists behind them as they walk backward, then for the West (and for advanced capitalism), the future is a point along a highway—in front of us, but utterly predictable and quotidian. When we get on the expressway, we already know its terminus (or our exit). And other than to get off, there's no real option—it is not a mistake that twenty years of commentators have fastened on (now exhausted) metaphors of highways for information society—the highways take us somewhere, opening up a path where, perhaps, none existed before, *but* they also block off other possibilities. As Marc Augé (1995) writes of "non-place," culture in the age of globalization is emptied of signification and difference, a tabula rasa upon which might be arranged the commodities that take the place of other cultural forms in the postmodern era. Traveling down the highway into the future, we know both where we're going and, courtesy of the proliferation of strip malls and fast food, what we'll find.

And what about anthropology in all of this? The current version of the culture wars, as David Palumbo-Liu (2002: 110) points out, resuscitates the long-discredited tradition of "national character" studies in anthropology in order to demonize middle-eastern peoples and to legitimate continued military and economic incursions into the region. In these works, "national interests seem indistinguishable from a 'way of life,' and national policy seems synonymous with large, civilizational imperatives." In other words, whole regions of the world can be characterized as violent or irrational, while the US and the West are represented as reasonable, tolerant, and scientific. The "future," such as it is, pits these groups against one another: the outcome will be a highly selective vision of "us" or "them" in a future that is more about the end of alternatives than their emergence.

As David Harvey (2000: 154) explains, the tragedy of the end of "utopic" thinking is precisely the truncation of the imagination to the hegemony of the "real": "If the mess seems impossible to change then it is simply because there is indeed 'no alternative.' It is the supreme rationality of the market versus the silly irrationality of anything else. And all those institutions that might have helped define some alternatives have either been suppressed or—with some notable exceptions, such as the church—brow-beaten into submission." A world where corporations and governments define the terms of the future is a world where the status quo will remain fundamentally unchallenged. What remains of utopias in the Western imaginary are what Louis Marin (1993) calls the "degenerate utopia": Disneyland, Celebration, Florida and the neighborhood shopping mall engage the utopian as the apotheosis of the commodity in what Walter Benjamin describes as the "hell" of the new (Buck-Morss 1989).

But while anthropology's ghosts continue to haunt conservative journalism and policy making, anthropologists have in the meantime cultivated a healthy skepticism for "culture" in the wake of its pervasive (and always already political) adoption in the public sphere. What has been erroneously labeled as the "anti-culturalist" camp looks to the formation of these bounded, cultural entities with suspicion, noting, after Eric Wolf, that "Names thus become things, and things marked with an X can become targets of war" (Wolf 1982: 7). What these contemporary approaches evidence is incredulity towards culture—in the very best sense. In the hands of cultural anthropologists, "culture" has been rendered adjectival—subordinated to more nominative analyses of power, class, race, and identity.

Moreover, "the future" isn't usually thought of as anthropology's purview. In fact, anthropologist's closest disciplinary neighbor—among those of us who are less concerned with anthropology qua science—is often thought to be history. As archaeologists or physical anthropologists, anthropologists may study a fossil record, a historical record, or an archaeological record. As cultural anthropologists, we may study contemporary society, but, until comparatively recently, through an "ethnographic present" with one methodological foot planted squarely in historicism. For example, Franz Boas's "culture history" called for the "reconstruction" of cultural development through an analysis of the diffusion of cultural elements (Mead 1959: 38).

In fact, anthropology has in many ways defined itself against an Arnoldian sense of culture as synonymous with progressive civilization. Indeed, Arnold's definition of culture was in many ways opposite of what anthropologists strive to understand—it eschewed what people actually did for what they *should* do—ultimately a kind of Platonic ideal.[3]

At any rate, the public, when they think of anthropology, tend to identify it with the study of small societies, "tribes," "communities"; the "anthropological gambit," after all, as Micaela di Leonardo (1998) terms it, has to do with the humorous juxtaposition of "the primitive" and "the civilized." The future will bring only more revelations of sameness and difference in a tableau vivant of savagery and civilization. However, a moment's reflection allows one to challenge this: neither of the terms in the anthropological gambit—"primitive" or "civilized"—is really true and anthropologists, far from being consigned to the study of the quaint or, at any rate, safely distant, cultural other, have long studied the contemporary present and, even, the future. After all, activist anthropology is precisely involved in producing future change. Acting to close down the College of the Americas (Gill 2004), or organizing graduate students at Yale (Kadir 2006) simultaneously advances a kind of cultural future, that is, a way of life less imbricated in violence and inequality. That is, nested in these critical exposés of violence and exploitation are other challenges to cultural mores overdetermining the domination of the weak by the powerful (for example, neoliberal emphases on "individualism" and "meritocracy").

But there's a more speculative side to this as well. Writing at a time when sociology and anthropology blurred together in various ways, H. G. Wells (1914: 205) wrote that "the creation of Utopias—and their exhaustive criticism—is the proper and distinctive method of sociology." Like sociology, nineteenth century anthropology was never far from utopian speculations about the future. The "savage" and "utopian" tropes arose together out of the Western imaginary, conceptions of the utopian future dialectically generated in changing ideas of the "savage" past (Trouillot 1991).

It was not until the twentieth century that cultural anthropologists would accede to a religiously synchronic "ethnographic present" disdainful of nineteenth century evolutionism, on the one hand, and utopian (or dystopian) speculation, on the other. But that does not mean that anthropologists gave up their purchase on the future. In fact, I would argue that the opposite is true: anthropological research in the cultural "present" is enabled by a relationship with historically specific *futures*. The history of these relationships has never been a part of the "ethnographer-as-hero" mythic cycle that anthropologists tell themselves (with the help of Susan Sontag); yet this work may demarcate both what and how anthropologists know.

In the twenty-first century, laying open these subcutaneous relationships has never been so important. As the future recedes to ever-more terrifying recapitulations of the present, the "anthropological gambit" itself is no longer an option for anthropologists. That is, it is no longer tenable (and, of course, never was) to argue, as Ruth Benedict did in *Patterns of Culture* (1934), that other peoples could be conceived as a "laboratory" for cultural differences. But we need—more than ever—to revisit the idea that anthropology might provide material and critique for cultural futures, for the imagination of different lifeways less premised on exploitation and ecological degradation. And not simply as an ancillary effect of anthropological research, either; I argue that raising the possibility for radical alterity is one of the chief roles of cultural anthropology in the twenty-first century.

Accordingly, this book has two major goals: (1) excavating anthropology's "future work" over the past two centuries and (2) suggesting where the future of thinking about the future may be (and may be heading) in anthropology. It in no way argues that anthropology should take up the dubious practice of cultural prediction. Rather, this book gradually develops the idea that anthropology's role is to gesture to radical alterity and, in turn, shift attention away from the inexorable tide of mass-produced homogeneity to divergent cultural practices and possibilities, not a self-legitimating cultural relativism that rationalizes the cultural other only as a prophylactic against cultural change and a blind behind which power can continue uncontested, but as the shocking revelation that difference begets difference. To take Gregory Bateson's famous dictum (1979) utterly out of context, we need to understand the cultural future as a difference that makes a difference. In other words, the future lies not in peddling the anthropological gambit of incommensurability, but in vouchsafing the possibility that ways in which we think and act may be very different in the future and in doing so, opening up a space (or a spacetime) for critical reflection on the present.

Chapter 1 begins with an examination of the future in nineteenth century anthropology, one enabled by a kind of cultural "time machine" (after the work of Johannes Fabian) that examined other peoples as existing in the past in order to provide clues for the future. And yet these temporal perambulations were fraught with paradox. An examination of the work of Alfred Russel Wallace, J. G. Frazer, E. B. Tylor, and others suggests the sorts of uneasiness of the nineteenth century future and also sets up the continuing problem for anthropology: how can culture simultaneously exist in past, present and future? What an examination of the nineteenth century suggests is the way time unravels under the anthropological gaze. The singularity of cultural comparison sets up conurbations of timelines and time paradoxes that continue to bedevil us today.

Chapters 2 and 3 center on Margaret Mead and Chad Oliver, whom I regard as the most important "apical ancestors" in our speculations on the future of culture. Mead wrote widely on every possible subject; there is no anthropologist alive today who wrote so broadly. And yet, one of the most important "Meads" that emerges is Mead the futurist, attempting to evoke radical alterity in her evocations of the future of culture, which, as she settles into her (self-appointed) role as in loco parentis to the counterculture, more and more favors youthful possibility over technocratic planning. Chapter 2 traces her development from a committed social engineer in her wartime work on morale with Gregory Bateson and her participation in the Josiah Macy conferences to her development of a model of cultural "microevolution" emphasizing becoming, complexity, and the unpredictable. Rather than dismiss Mead's later work (as many anthropologists have), I revisit it in order to unearth Mead's growing predilections for a future that cannot be engineered, a position in many ways anticipating emphases on the "emergent" in anthropological studies of science and technology.

Chad Oliver never had the same cachet as Mead—he lived the (comparatively) quiet life of Chair of the Department of Anthropology at the University of Texas during much of his professional career; he is better known for his anthropological science fiction than for his scholarly output and is regarded as one of the founders of that subgenre (along with Alfred Kroeber's more famous daughter, Ursula K. Le Guin). Utilizing stories and archival materials, I look to the overlaps between Oliver's science fiction and his anthropology, building to the general interrogation of anthropology as a colonial project and leading to Oliver's contribution to science fiction's "New Wave" in the 1960s. The end of Oliver's life sees him groping for different direction in both science fiction and anthropology as a way beyond the pessimism he saw in both projects by the end of the twentieth century.

Chapters 4 and 5 look to the legacies of Mead and Oliver for anthropologists in the 1970s and 1980s. Chapter 4 examines the search for extraterrestrials as an elaboration on the anthropological engagement with the

Other through the work of anthropologists in dialogue with NASA, SETI (the Search for Extraterrestrial Intelligence), and other institutions involved in searching for and theorizing about extraterrestrial life. I suggest that this fascination with the "ultimate" Other is also a kind of speculation on the future of the human. Chapter 5, on the other hand, is concerned with the ways anthropologists have engaged in the "official" practice of cultural futurism, that is, those theories and methods associated with the work of futurists. Never central to a field dominated by political scientists and sociologists, anthropologists have nonetheless contributed a window onto alternative futures based on the experiences of both non-Western and ordinary peoples removed from the pundits and power elite who make up the usual interlocutors for futurists. Among other things, these evocations of cultural futures break us out of what Robert Textor has called "tempocentrism": "To one's being unduly centered in one's own temporality" (Textor 1995a: 522). Ultimately, anthropological approaches can do even more; by questioning "tempocentrism," an anthropology of cultural futures calls "our" temporality into question. Do we really live in the homogenous, progressive chronotype of the modern, or, as Bruno Latour (1993) has questioned in another context, is this another case where "we have never been modern"?

Chapters 6 and 7 evaluate anthropological future work in a present, a time where "the future" itself is bracketed away. Under conditions of speedup, the future becomes proleptic, that is, it seeps into the present moment as "emergent" phenomena. Many anthropologists have fastened on emergent phenomena as a way of inserting anthropological voices into rapidly changing areas in science and technology—for example, genetics and reproduction—and intervening in order to create more equitable cultural futures. And yet, this race to the new may in the end turn Pyrrhic; what is construed as "emergent" may turn out to be a dull recapitulation of the past, that is, the "novel" rather than the "new." These last chapters address the possibility of the truly "new" construed as cultural changes involving new formations of power and knowledge that utterly change our conceptions of ourselves and others. Despite a long history of future work, we have yet to harness the critical potentials of anthropological futures. In the final chapter I trace the possibility of an "open" future as ultimately suggestive of both the critical new and representing the best opportunity for an anthropology of the future.

In all of these chapters, I have (mostly) resisted the urge to insert my own future work which has ranged broadly from simulations (Collins 2006a) and the application of Delphi methods to the emergence of "cyborg" identities in multiagent systems composed of human and non-human agents (Collins 2006b; Collins and Trajkovski 2006). My own experiences have both confronted me with my own tempocentrisms while at the same time convincing me of the (mostly) untapped critical potentials of the future as a site for cultural alterity. In this I have been aided by what I have come to think of as "theorists of the new," that is, the philosopher Henri Bergson and his latter-day apologists Gilles Deleuze, Keith Ansell-Pearson, and Elizabeth Grosz. But I would argue that their relevance to anthropology lies less in grafting their theory onto anthropology than in using their ideas to recognize what was anthropological all along. Like them, though, it is my hope and expectation that the future brings with it the utterly unanticipated; it is, after all, in the context of surprise and shock that we have the best opportunity for imagining alternatives to the present.

Although anthropology is usually thought of as a "time machine" taking people back through time by the study of the Other, a better image of anthropology might be as a temporal anomaly where the many specious "spacetimes" of nineteenth century cultural anthropology collide in a flash that undermines exactly what we think we mean by "past," "present," and "future." But this means a tantalizing, even surrealistic, evocation rather than a prognostication, designed as much to unsettle what we think we know as to gesture toward what will be. Ultimately, what that future might look like must remain unknown; this is the promise of culture conceived anthropologically.

NOTES

Parts of this introduction have been previously published as "Sail On! Sail On! Anthropology, Science Fiction and the Enticing Future," *Science Fiction Studies* 30(2) (2003): 180–98. The author would like to thank the publication for permission to use the material here.

1. That is, the "Moore's Law" attributed to Gordon Moore, the cofounder of Intel, which, in the halcyon days of the 1990s, became a rallying cry for venture capital in Silicon Valley.
2. Francis Fukuyama's *The End of History and the Last Man* (1992) elaborates on his idea that "liberal democracy" constitutes the endpoint of historical development (at least in his highly selective version of Hegelian dialectic).
3. And yet, by emphasizing the integrative character of culture, many anthropologists in the twentieth century were (however unintentionally) echoing the Arnoldian project by outlining a "modal personality" to which members of society should conform.

Chapter 1

Anthropological Time Machines: Setting the Controls for the Future

In H. G. Wells's *The Time Machine* (1895), we glimpse a world 800,000 years in the future where Homo sapiens have speciated in the Eloi and the Morlocks, with the Eloi leading a Dionysian existence on the Earth's surface and the Morlocks dwelling in subterranean lairs, only emerging to prey on the fragile, mercurial Eloi. Both species, however, are the end products of the steady progress of humanity—a cautionary tale for an age overwhelmingly confident of the salutary effects of science and technology. As the Time Traveller explains:

> I grieved to think how brief the dream of the human intellect had been. It had committed suicide. It had set itself steadfastly towards comfort and ease, a balanced society with security and permanency as its watchword, it had attained its hopes—to come to this at last. Once, life and property must have reached almost absolute safety. The rich had been assured of his wealth and comfort, the toiler assured of his life and work. No doubt in that perfect world there had been no unemployment problem, no social question left unsolved. And a great quiet followed. (Wells 1895).

Having attained the utopian promise of progress—freedom from want, safety, et cetera.—humanity stagnates into etiolated shadows of its former (European) self. As Thomas Huxley's student, Wells was as qualified as any to engage in this kind of evolutionary speculation and, in doing so, reinvents the utopia for the modern age (qua dystopia). But however well the Time Traveller's time machine works, Wells's time machine could use some adjustment.

The Time Machine purports to take us far into the future along a singular path set with the Time Traveller's levers. But it doesn't seem to work like that. For one thing, the Eloi and Morlocks belong not to the future, but to the (Victorian) present. As Cantor and Hufnagel (2006: 36) note, "Wells's many false starts and the number of versions he went through before he published *The Time Machine* as we know it is testament to the difficulty of his enterprise. It is therefore understandable that when he was trying to imagine a journey into the future, he ended up modeling it on something more familiar, a journey to the imperial frontier." Thus, the degenerate species he encounters represent both class conflict in, say, Benjamin Disraeli's London, and the cultural Other, with the Time Traveller as Joseph Conrad's Marlow or H. Rider Haggard's Quatermain. And the Time Traveller's perambulations in the future are themselves imbricated in the past, beginning with the shock of the new, but, by degrees, descending both spatially (into the Morlock's lair) and chronologically, through dusty ruins and broken machinery to a museum of nineteenth century Britain. Finally, the flowers the Time Traveller carries in his pocket are proof, on the one hand, of the reality of the future, but equally proof of the future in the present. The problem of Wells's future, I would suggest, is that it is poisoned by anachronism, while the present is distorted by prolepsis. The Time Traveller's otherwise superfluous trip to the very end of time makes more sense with this in mind; only by standing at the terminal point of all of these temporal anomalies can the Time Traveller grasp the whole—to understand the suture, he must step outside of this sullied time stream altogether. It is this that makes *The Time Machine* more of a utopia.

The following chapter explores the future as one of the nagging concerns of nineteenth century anthropology. What the aforementioned thoughts on Wells suggest, though, is that the future is not objective, linear, and Cartesian, but cultural and heterogeneous, heir to post-Newtonian temporalities.[1] Sorting out the strands of this thoroughly discombobulated future (and past) emerges as anthropology's task, namely E. B. Tylor's "reformer's science." To work things out these anthropologists will need a time machine, but, as Wells and the genre of time travel he founded teach us, the time machine is like Derrida's *pharmakon,* both cure and poison at the same time. Time continues to bedevil anthropology for many reasons, not the least of which is its strange half-life in anthropological theory where, like Wells's Time Traveller, spatial movement fills in for (and defers) temporal movement. In the end, it is the anthropologist who doesn't know where (or when) she's going.

It has been nearly forty years since the publication of Johannes Fabian's *Time and the Other* (1983), a scathing indictment of temporal distortions—what Fabian calls "allochronism"—that have overdetermined the anthropological encounter, the time machine that informed racist anthropology.[2] But this time machine was no mere epiphenomena of the racism of the time;

"allochronism" enabled the anthropological project well into the twentieth century. That is, the multiplication of timescapes was both problem and solution for Victorian anthropology. We can see the quixotic methodology at its most developed in Sir James Frazer, the last of the great, "armchair" anthropologists of the nineteenth century. Struck by a temporal distortion—the "barbarity" of the "priesthood of Nemi"—Frazer (1922) begins his own time tripping through a kaleidoscope of pasts, presents, and futures in order to get the chronologies right:

> The strange rule of this priesthood has no parallel in classical antiquity, and cannot be explained from it. To find an explanation we must go farther outside. No one will probably deny that such a custom savours of a barbarous age, and, surviving into imperial times, stands out in striking isolation from the polished Italian society of the day, like a primaeval rock rising from a smooth-shaven lawn. It is the very rudeness and barbarity of the custom which allow us a hope of explaining it. For recent researches into the early history of man have revealed the essential similarity with which, under many superficial differences, the human mind has elaborated its first crude philosophy of life. Accordingly, if we can show that a barbarous custom, like that of the priesthood of Nemi, has existed elsewhere; if we can detect the motives which led to its institution; if we can prove that these motives have operated widely, perhaps universally, in human society, producing in varied circumstances a variety of institutions specifically different but generically alike; if we can show, lastly, that these motives, with some of their derivative institutions, were actually at work in classical antiquity; then we may fairly infer that at a remoter age the same motives gave birth to the priesthood of Nemi.

For Frazer, as for E. B. Tylor, Lewis Henry Morgan, Otis Mason, and others, typological comparisons of putatively "primitive" peoples granted anthropologists an insight into the origins of European civilization. "Systematic study of the 'primitive' first began in hopes of using them as a kind of time machine, a peep into our own past, as providing closer evidence about the early links in the great Series" (Fabian 1983: 39). For Frazer (1922), this meant a glimpse into the shadowy origins of magic and religion; for Morgan (1877), examinations of the kinship systems of Native American peoples allowed him to explore the origin of the American nuclear family. Since Europeans were thought to have passed through a stage sequence en route to civilization (most famously Morgan's triptych of "savagery," "barbarism," and "civilization"), it followed that the study of contemporary "savages" and "barbarians" would allow anthropologists to speculate on European development by analogy. Anthropologists have (retrospectively) termed this comparative method "unilinear evolutionary theory." But were these temporal perambulations so simple? And what about the safety of the Time Traveller?

Aren't we worried about the butterfly effect? It's worth asking what these traipses into the cultural past may have (unintentionally) done to cultures of the future.

In the mythologies anthropologists tell themselves (cf. Handler 1990; Stocking 1992), "unilinear evolutionism" and the pernicious variants of social Darwinism that it perpetuated gave way to the synchronic study of cultures as integrated wholes (culture history, functionalism, structural-functionalism) and then, by the end of the twentieth century, to the (re)integration of the cultural Other into our own, historical time, complete with its savage inequalities wrought by war, imperialism, and globalization. "Other time" has, in this account, been superseded by another chronotype—"global time"—which, according to David Harvey (1989), has supplanted space as an organizing trope altogether.

But this seems too easy: a linear account documenting the demise of "unlinear" theory. The problem is that "unlinear evolutionary theory" was never particularly linear to begin with, and failing to appreciate this insight may push us into a closed time loop where we give birth to our own colonizing discourse.[3] The achievements of the Victorian time machine rested on a heterogeneous simultaneity of time effects that were, at the very least, incommensurate, and, at their worst, positively contradictory, what Fabian (1983: 21) calls the "schizogenic use of Time." Having distorted the past in their errant quest for European origins, the "future" likewise threatens to unravel.

PROGRESS AS A "DIFFERENCE" ENGINE

Time for much of the pre-Enlightenment world is thought have been cyclic; in fact, this has been the primary rationale for anthropologists spending at least one year in the field—to gain a sense of the ebb and flow of the seasons that were supposed to make up the ever present of the small society. This is in contrast to what might be called "biblical time," the descent of the Fall and the uneven climb to salvation (cf. Trigger 1998). Yet, neither of these chronotypes would be sufficient for an Enlightenment founding its science on the isolation of time as a variable: "Hence it could not become part of a Cartesian system of time-space coordinates allowing the scientists to plot a multitude of *uneventful* data over neutral time, unless it was first naturalized, i.e., separated from events meaningful to mankind" (Fabian 1983: 14). Initiated by philosophe encyclopaedists like Diderot, this "naturalization" was not fully achieved until Lyell and Darwin. This was Darwin's breakthrough, especially with regards to human evolution: the neutralization of time as a succession of stages in human becoming. Time was not immanent; it was merely a table through which statistical distributions of traits were expressed.

Ironically, the older, biblical time would seem more salubrious to native peoples subjected to colonial rule under the British. Pre-Darwinist groups like the Aborigines Protection Society (and, later, the Ethnological Society of London) may have ethnocentrically measured the cultural Other against British civilization but, in the alembic of Christian conversion, even the rudest savage would emerge as *ab uno sanguine:*

> But the protectors of aborigines and the London ethnologists did *not* advocate the interests of the people studied except in the latter's capacity as *the (to be) converted.* But the APS and the ESL conceived of their objects as temporal beings subject to missionary interventions. Therefore they defined them in terms of conversion: as possessing a past to be studied and salvaged and a present and future in which they would be turned into religiously and/or secularly civilized beings. (Pels 1999: 105)

That is, however "savage" peoples under British control were, all cultural (and temporal) differences were subtended beneath biblical time, a common chronology stretching between the Fall and the coming of the Paraclete: *ab uno tempore.* Ironically, cleaving "time" from its Christian significations also had the effect—in the hands of anthropologists—of excising "other" time from "our" time.

As Fabian says, it fell to anthropologists, contre Darwin, to resignify "neutral time," to, as it were, turn Darwin on his head and create a chronopolitical grid that facilitated comparisons between cultures. But this was no easy task; the challenge was to construe the cultural Other according to heterogeneous spacetimes that were somehow still connected to one another, that is, the separation and simultaneous conjoining of multiple pasts, presents, and futures. The confusion starts with nineteenth century anthropology's apical ancestor: Herbert Spencer.

One of the breakthroughs of the Enlightenment (or the late Renaissance, depending upon whom you read) was the invention of progress, a concept utterly foreign to a medieval worldview premised on theodicy and eschatology. Progress, on the other hand, promised that past and present institutions and practices would be succeeded by more rational, more perfect forms, an idea that, for Enlightenment philosophers, as Bruce Trigger (1998: 41) suggests, "forged a powerful basis for legitimating their critiques of existing institutions and demanding that they be reformed." Expanding on this, Herbert Spencer argued that progress was a natural law of the universe, moving ineluctably from simple to complex, from homogeneous to heterogeneous, and from concrete to abstract, and was as evident in cosmology as it was in the proliferation of Earth's biota (Kiernan 2002: 15).

This conception of progress was, of course, quite at odds with Darwin and with the growing dominance of Darwinism, which, as Joseph Fracchia and R.C. Lewontin (1999: 61) explain, developed a theory of variation "causally random with respect to the external forces that influence the maintenance and spread of those variations in the population." That is to say, human variation was non-teleogical; there was nothing ineluctable—or even uniform—about evolution. Although some unilinear apologists have defended nineteenth century anthropologists against this imminence (Carneiro 2003: 16), it seems clear that progress itself *was* a theory of imminence, one that to the nineteenth century mind indicated not only the direction of human development, but also its ultimate ends: "the creation of earthly perfection" (Trigger 1998: 61).

While there may have been numerous challenges to theories of imminence over the course of successive elaborations in natural selection (Gould 1981), with respect to anthropology imminence continued, coiled about theories of biological evolution. We can see this in the "excluded ancestor" (Handler 2000) of Alfred Russel Wallace, the codiscoverer of natural selection who, in a burst of altruistic magnanimity unknown in science today, remanded full credit to Charles Darwin, who, in some ways, was to remain in Wallace's debt for the rest of his career. Having developed the idea, however, Wallace found natural selection in many ways an inadequate explanation for evolution, particularly in the case of humans who, he felt, had "transcended" the mechanism of natural selection altogether. In his landmark 1864 paper, "The Origins of Human Races Deduced From the Theory of Natural Selection," he makes the case for this human exceptionalism, his imagination turning from the mystery of humanity's origins to its ultimate ends:

> In concluding this brief sketch of the great subject, I would point out its bearing on the future of the human race. If my conclusions are just, it must inevitably follow that the higher—the more intellectual and moral—must displace the lower and more degraded races; and the power of "natural selection," still acting on his mental organization, must ever lead to the more perfect adaptation of man's higher faculties to the conditions of surrounding nature, and to the exigencies of the social state. While his external form will probably ever remain unchanged, except for the development of that perfect beauty which results from a healthy and well-organized body, refined and ennobled by the highest intellectual faculties and sympathetic emotions, his mental constitution may continue to advance and improve till the world is again inhabited by a single homogeneous race, no individual of which will be inferior to the noblest specimens of existing humanity. Each one will then work out his own happiness in relation to

that of his fellows; perfect freedom of action will be maintained, since the well balanced moral faculties will never permit anyone to transgress on the equal freedom of others; restrictive laws would not be wanted, for each man will be guided by the best of laws; a thorough appreciation of the rights, and a perfect sympathy of the feelings, of all about him; compulsory government will have died away as unnecessary (for every man will know how to govern himself), and will be replaced by voluntary associations for all within those limits which most conduce to happiness; and mankind will at length have discovered that it was only required of them to develop the capacities of their higher nature, in order to convert the Earth, which had so long been the theatre of their unbridled passions and the scene of unimaginable misery, into as bright a paradise as ever haunted the dreams of seer or poet.

Wallace's conclusions angered some in attendance at the Anthropological Society of London meeting, including the polygenist James Hunt, who "demanded that Wallace withdraw his 'beautiful dream' of humanity's future, which had nothing to do with his theory of humanity's origins or the theory of natural selection" (quoted in Slotten 2004: 214). However out of pace such speculation might have been with Darwin's theories (and it was not, really; Darwin had offered more guarded prognostications in *Descent of Man*), Wallace's speculative leaps form the Ur-text for an anthropology with one foot in Spencer and the other in Darwin, each approach splitting anthropological futures into separate time loops from which anthropologists continue to strive to break free.

Some of these loops include:

Humanity's Unified Future: What angered many of Wallace's critics was his insistence on the "psychic unity" of humanity, especially as polygenism was reborn as eugenics in the last decades of the nineteenth century. For Wallace, perhaps because (as Peter Pels has suggested) of his own, humble origins, together with his anthropological fieldwork in Malaysia, humans may have differed in many ways, but were being guided along the same path, not by natural selection but, as his involvement in Spiritualism deepened, by "spiritual intervention" (Pels 2003: 255).

Humanity's Relative Futures: Progress may have been universal, but its expression in different races, nationalities, and cultures varied considerably. This part of Wallace was implicit in the talk of "higher" and "lower" races, and is the racist underside to a theorist who, compared to many of his contemporaries, was amazingly progressive. Jackson, together with Francis Galton and many others, may have developed Spencer's "survival of the fittest" into a full-blown program of social Darwinism, but Wallace's Owenite egalitarianism was still grounded in the idea that the "lower" races would naturally become extinct, an idea quite at odds with his insistence that the role of the colonial was to "civilize" subjected peoples. But this made perfect sense in the logic of Frazer's time machine, where "savage races are not on the same plane, but have stopped or tarried in the upward path" (Frazer, quoted in Carneiro 2003: 19). As Morgan (quoted in Haller 1971: 718) put it, "those savage societies which were still in their low stage of development would surely make advancements in time, but unfortunately, they would be forever distanced by the progress of more advanced peoples."

But even this does not capture the near-Einsteinian deployment of time in nineteenth century anthropology. Spencer's theory of "recapitulation"—that species progress was repeated at the level of ontogeny—proved popular with educators and the nascent science of developmental psychology in addition to anthropology. As Egan Kiernan (2002: 18–19) explains,

> Spencer believed that the child's experience was like that of our distant ancestors faced by the phenomenon around them and trying to comprehend them. Over the ages of active struggle with the material features of their lives, of speculation and experiment, human beings have gradually reached our current understanding. The mind of a young child similarly faces the puzzle of the world, and children follow a similar route by similar procedures in coming to a modern understanding.

Spencer's recapitulation was, accordingly, recapitulated by countless anthropologists (and other colonials) who pronounced that the savage mind was like that of a child, in Lucien Lévy-Bruhl's formulation, a "pre-logical" mentality paralleled in Piaget's developmental schema and Freud's "omnipotence of thoughts" (Styers 2004: 134–135). "Civilized" children, then, raced through the stages of savagery and barbarism to the status so difficultly attained by the non-European. A contemporary sense of this (racist) relativity lies in the often-repeated axiom that time races ahead in globalized metropoles while slowing to a trickle in the developing peripheries.

TEMPORAL ANOMALIES

While the idea of different cultures existing in different bubbles of time moving at different speeds of cultural development was certainly consonant with Tylor's and Morgan's classificatory approach, it presented certain problems, namely the integrity of the individuated time continuums. Tylor codified this into a doctrine of "survivals," atavistic, irrational customs and behaviors that were relics of previous planes of cultural space-time. Temporal atavisms were, accordingly, drags on cultural progress and, for the anthropologist, targets for extirpation. As Tylor (1958: vol. II, 539) wrote in *Primitive Culture:* "It is a harsher, and at times even painful, office of ethnography to expose the remains of crude old culture which have passed into harmful superstition, and to mark them out for destruction. Yet this work, if less genial, is not the less urgently needed for the good of mankind. Thus, active at once in aiding progress and in removing hindrance, the science of culture is essentially a reformer's science." But what was marked out for "reform"? For Tylor, anachronisms ranged from the trivial (clothing that bore the vestiges of earlier ages) to what he considered to be outdated superstitions in Britain. He reserved special outrage, however, for putatively "primitive" customs flourishing among Britain's middle classes, for example the growth of Spiritualism in the last decades of the nineteenth century. As Peter Pels (2003) has recounted, Tylor and Wallace sparring over the existence of the spirit world made for exciting press in Victorian times, with Wallace challenging Tylor to attend a séance with him. Wallace, for his part, took Rousseau's tactic, holding up the civilized behavior of the Malays he studied and castigating Britain for its manifest inequality (Pels 2003: 259). And Morgan laid into Mormons for practicing what he believed to be atavistic, polygamous marriage.

So here, caught in the gears of the Victorian time machine, we have heterogeneous times. On the one hand, a Eurocentric time masquerading as universal, pan-human time; the time of technological progress, of civilization and rationality. On the other, local eddies of time, swirling centrifugally, impotently, back to their source. But time travel only works if there is some possibility of connection between these different space-times—a time machine. But, having forged the wormholes to connect them, one continually threatens to collapse into the other. As Paul Cantor and Peter Hufnagel (2006: 53) note of Wells's time machine, "The raw materials of the time machine are the raw materials of empire, exactly the minerals and other valuable substances brought back from the frontier to supply the industrial and technological needs of Europe." What if European time depended upon "savage" and "barbaric" time for its field integrity? What if the "time of progress" depended upon (rather than transcended) the savage times that were sited outside of it? Indeed, Bergson mounts a similar critique of other false chronologies—for example, the idea that "non-being" precedes "being": "Being, order or the existence are truth itself; but in the false problem there is a fundamental illusion, a 'retrograde movement of the true,' according to which being, order, and the existent are supposed to precede themselves, or to precede the creative act that constitutes them, by projecting an image of themselves back into a possibility, a disorder, a nonbeing which are supposed to be primordial" (Deleuze 1991: 18). The time machine, in other words, creates more problems than it solves, founded from the outset on the classic time paradox (explored, for example, in Robert Heinlein's "All You Zombies"), the West giving birth to itself through the "retrograde" creation of its own conditions of overcoming, as it were. Given the initial paradox, how can any anthropologist keep these time-space continua distinct?

BOAS AND THE REFORMER'S SCIENCE

It would be a mistake to claim that unilinear evolutionism ended with the nineteenth century. To begin with, it continued into the twentieth century (and into our present) in a thousand different forms. For example, Christopher Roth (2005: 73) points out that Theosophy (the heir to Spiritualism and the ancestor to several UFO-centered religions) reinscribed the "psychic unity" of the early nineteenth century in the succession of "root races." Benjamin Lee Whorf was, in fact, one of its most ardent believers, arguing "that America would be the home of the Coming Race, its destiny assured by the subtle infusion of Amerindian blood into a largely European-dominated gene pool" (Roth 2005: 73).[4]

But these "survivals" aside, Franz Boas is nevertheless credited—in US anthropology, at least—with finally burying the unilinear evolutionism of the nineteenth century, mostly by insisting that any universalist "laws" of cultural development be supported with empirical data and real histories, rather than the just-so stories that were the basis for Victorian anthropology (Pierpoint 2004; Stocking 1987, 1992). And Boas did these things; mounting a sustained attack on the centers of racist anthropology (at that time, Harvard and the Smithsonian), Boas established a vision of professional (and ethical) anthropology that has persisted until now. But it would be a mistake to say that Boas left evolutionary time entirely. George Stocking (1992: 110) notes that "Boas never abandoned entirely a nineteenth century liberal belief in human progress." And for good reasons. Without the progressive metanarrative, what hope was there for the future? To reject all evolutionary timelines was to admit that history was "one damn thing after another" and, as Trigger (1998: 226) elaborates, "to deny the possibility of genuine progress and therefore of overcoming deep-seated problems and creating a better type of society than has ever existed before." Instead, Boas, together with the erstwhile Boasians, deferred Spencerian progress along a separate temporal axis. As Margaret Mead—who oftentimes seems to remember a very different Boas than, say, Robert Lowie—writes of Boas's conceptualization of the *long duree* of human progress: "Within this great panorama Boas saw the scientific task as one of progressive probing into a problem now of language, now of physical type, now of art style, each a deep, sudden, intensive stab at some strategic point into an enormous untapped and unknown mass of information which we would someday master. No probe must go too far lest it lead to premature generalizations, a development which he feared like the plague and against which he continually warned us" (Mead 1959: 31). Given the paucity of empirical data, what is known retrospectively as the "Boasian school" eschewed broad generalizations and specious comparisons for more local studies, but without jettisoning evolutionary time. Or, rather, by sublimating one kind of evolutionary time (the identification of local pockets of cultural space-time) under the progressive aegis of another (the triumphant march of scientific progress).

All of these quantum threads collide in Boas's most well-known public intellectual work, *Anthropology of Modern Life,* where, continuing the conceit, he tries to repair the Victorian time machine and, rather like the character of Sam in the television series, *Quantum Leap,* "fix that which was broken." But meddling in one chronotype invariably generates paradox in another timeline.

Boas rejects the idea that anthropology should accede to the status of a predictive science. For him, universal laws of human development were too lofty a goal for a science still establishing its proper method. And besides, culture change does not take place in discrete stages; culture changes according to its own, aberrant, Heisenberg principle:

> Here, as well as in other social phenomena, accident cannot be eliminated, accident that may depend upon the presence or absence of eminent individuals, upon the favors bestowed by nature, upon chance discoveries or contacts, and therefore prediction is precarious, if not impossible. (Boas 2004: 246)

In other words, not being able to say exactly where culture has been, Boas is not sanguine of the ability to prognosticate on its future.

But having rejected Tylor's vision, Boas (217–218) still acknowledges a form of Spencerian progress, albeit grudgingly:

> Thus we may recognize progress in a definite direction in the development of invention and knowledge. If we should value a society entirely on the basis of its technical and scientific achievements it would be easy to establish a line of progress which, although not uniform, leads from simplicity to complexity.

And he is even (218), after a fashion, willing to admit a certain line of progress in society:

> In earlier times, among ourselves, the status of noblemen, or the serf, or even a member of the guild, was fixed by birth; that of a priest by the authority of

the church. For most of us there are still two forms of status that entail serious obligation and that persist unless the status is changed by authority of the
State. These are citizenship and marriage. The latter status shows now strong
evidence of weakening. In the sense of loss of fixity of status the freedom of the
individual has been increasing.

All of this begs the question, of course, of which timespace Boas is describing—is that "our" time? Are "they" included? In *Anthropology of Modern Life,*
Boas and his audience were all contained in that first timestream, what Marshall Sahlins (1960) would later rationalize as "general" evolution. In *Anthropology,* it's not clear what time anthropology's interlocutors inhabit. Native
Americans and others provide numerous ethnographic examples that rela-
tivize, that is, call into question the universality of Western cultural mores,
but they are not adduced as Europe's past. The theory of infinite universes?

And as with the anthropologists that preceded Boas, progress stumbles
against anachronistic customs, threatening to suck the advances of science
down a time vortex: "It is, however, worth noting that notwithstanding the
decided breakdown of belief in tradition, strong traditions persist" (Boas
2004: 79), including racism and nationalism, vestiges of the past that the
Boasians hoped would disappear in a more progressive age.

> It follows that the "instinctive" race antipathy can be broken down, if we suc-
> ceed in creating among young children social groups that are not divided ac-
> cording to principles of race and which have principles of cohesion that weld
> the group into a whole. (79–80)

Like Tylor, Boas saw the anthropological project as a "reformer's science,"
but without Tylor's self-congratulatory tone. Extirpating still extant pockets
of ignorance would not, in itself, bring about a utopian society, but would
lay the groundwork for a recursive process of skeptical inquiry that would
result in real progress. This was the biggest different between these twin
projects of reform. For Tylor, the end of anthropological critique would be
the universalization of the British, bourgeois order, for Boas (200–201), it
would mean overcoming that order:

> Whatever our generation may achieve will attain in the course of time that
> venerable respect that will lay in chains in the minds of our successors, and it
> will require new efforts to free a future generation of the shackles that we are
> forging. When we once recognize this process, we must see that it is our task not
> only to free ourselves of traditional prejudice, but also to search in the heritage
> of the past for what is useful and right, and to endeavor to free the mind of
> future generations so that they may not cling to our mistakes but may be ready
> to correct them.

This would be a theme that Boasians like Benedict and Mead would take up in earnest, in some ways turning the Victorian time machine on its head. Other cultural mores were not to be understood as existing in the West's past, but in its future. That is, an understanding of other cultures both de-naturalized our understanding of our own, while at the same time opening the mind to cultural alternatives that might serve as a catalyst for change in the future. But, like its nineteenth century ancestor, the direction of this change was also mapped out. As Boas (184) wrote, "the whole history of mankind points in a direction of a *human* ideal as opposed to a *national* ideal." Boas reintroduced *moral* time into the continuum; the end-time that modernity gestured to was also a time of justice, hearkening back to the biblical time of a pre-Darwinian age. But it fell to Boas's heirs, however, to work out these timelines.

In the final months of 1939, many of the Boasians (and many other anthropologists) enjoined the fight against fascism; Stocking (1992: 165) claims that 75 percent of anthropologists were involved in some capacity (cf. Price 1998). Margaret Mead, Ruth Benedict, and Gregory Bateson began their war efforts with the "Committee on National Morale"—an effort to engineer *esprit de theme* among the citizenry, although Bateson used these same techniques to help fuel the Southeast Asia propaganda machine (Howard 1984; Price 1998). Later, the Boasians would contribute "national character" studies of Allied and Axis powers in order to promote intercultural cooperation (among Allies) and maximize dissension (among Axis powers). Bateson contributed notes on Nazi film, while Geoffrey Gorer (1943) famously urged the Allies not to execute the Japanese emperor.

But the best-known work produced during this period was Ruth Benedict's *The Chrysanthemum and the Sword* (1946), a far-ranging study of Japanese national character utilizing imprisoned Japanese Americans as informants, together with Japanese film and key texts. The result was a blend of cultural studies and applied anthropology, with prescriptions for changing Japanese society appearing alongside expositions of national characteristics like "honor," "hierarchy," et cetera. Of course, changing Japanese society was imagined from the position of the conqueror—that is, changing it to better resemble what Benedict believed to be key characteristics of the United States, "adopting the free and easy human contacts to which we are accustomed in the United States, the imperative demand to be independent, the passion each individual has to choose his own mate, his own job, the house he will live in and the obligations he will assume" (Benedict 1946: 314; Shannon 1995). However, to say that these traits were to be pressed upon the Japanese would smack too much of the nineteenth century anthropology the Boasians were distancing themselves from. Instead, Benedict, in a sleight-of-hand worthy of a seasoned time traveler, located these traits within Japanese culture itself: "For example, the two symbols that Benedict marshals for the title of the book—*The Chrysanthemum and the Sword*—symbolize both the pathologies and the promise of Japan in the postwar era. The chrysanthemum could become a symbol of individual freedoms in Japan, while the sword, however steeped in militarism, could also become a symbol of advanced *civitas*" (Shannon 1995: 411). In contrast with Benedict's earlier *Patterns of Culture* (1934), the Japanese need not be hemmed in by their "Apollonian" culture complex; instead, building dialectically on extant predilections, Japan could rejoin the "time" of the West, now reconceptualized as both a moral and a scientific time, like the United Nations and Greenwich Mean Time.

It goes without saying, perhaps, that much of the work of applied anthropology moves under the same time; interventions of all kinds are mapped onto a future conceived as a time for overcoming problems in the present. In the post-War era of W. W. Rostow, this time was—quite explicitly—the time of the US; later anthropologists would learn to dissociate "development" and the "United States." The time of progress became at once more moral and more Hegelian—progress would flow out of existing configurations. However, the end for all concerned was a moral coevalness.

GLOBALIZATION: THE ALWAYS ALREADY FUTURE

Whatever perspective we take on globalization—as victim of World Trade Organization (WTO) policy, consumer of clothing made in sweatshops stretching from Los Angeles to Karachi, academic commentator, et cetera—its pervasive influence draws us into a Skinnerian box which prevents us from considering other modalities. That is, "globalization"—the "shrinking" world, the multiplication of networks and nodes, the replacement of space by time (Harvey 1989), the "end of history"—all of these stretch into the distant future, an endless horizon of capitalism that may accelerate, proliferate, and intensify, but which is never going to end; we may be caught in a vortex of its "speed" (Virilio 1986). In this formulation, the production of the new is of crucial importance, if by that we mean the acceleration of *novelty*. That is, "newer," "faster," and more "fashionable" commodities and ways of life must be perceived to succeed one another in time. But this is not, strictly speaking, change at all. Your ketchup is replaced by one "twice as thick"; your car replaced by a roomier or more stylish one. Yet nothing at all has changed. Much of the marketing strategy for Advanced Information Technologies (AIT) hinges on them being perceived by consumers as *already* in the future. As I write now, high-definition television is just one such site for future chicanery.

This is especially problematic for anthropology. Even parts of the world more recently absorbed into global capitalism are not so much experiencing a "rupture" of the new than their inevitable and foreordained entrée into neo-liberal hegemony. When McDonald's opens in Cracow, Moscow, Chengdu, it hardly engenders surprise—just a quick nod to the inevitability of it all. Could Mogadishu be far behind? Thus the discourses of globalization at once purport to both describe the present, predict the future, and explain the past: testament to the sweeping power of free market ideologies.

And yet, this sense of homogeneous space and time is illusory for several reasons. As Anna Tsing (2000) has pointed out, there is no "globalization" without the local; the heterogeneous is the a priori condition for the homogeneous. In addition, it is not true that even the most "pure" globalization is free from closed time loops and temporal paradox. Like the nineteenth century evolutionary discourse to which it is heir, globalization is riven with discontinuous space time. Financial arbitrage, derivatives of all sorts, futures trading, risk management, rolling over short-term debt to finance long-term loans, betting against national currencies in order to trigger a cascading devaluation: these are different loops of time, the varying timescapes of global capitalism (Bestor 2004). These loops overlay anthropology's older time machines, overdetermining our encounters with these neo-liberal colonizations of the future. Like Wells's Time Traveller traversing museum galleries in the underground lair of the Morlocks, we travel to the future only to descend into the past. I submit that taking on the "timescapes" of the present means unraveling these (quantum) strings.

NOTES

1. There is a wide literature on the anthropology of time, which the present book does not purport to cover (cf. Gell 1992; Mann 1992). The irony, of course, is that anthropological sensitivities to the other times rarely seem as sensitive to the "time of the other," that is, the table (after Foucault) upon which our chronotypes are constructed.

2. That is to say, "racist" both in terms of its denigrating descriptions of nonwhites and for its role in the production of race *tout ensemble*.

3. This refers to the classic tale of time paradox, Robert Heinlein's "All You Zombies," where the protagonist goes back in time to give birth to himself (Heinlein 1959).

4. Benjamin Lee Whorf was by all accounts a Boasian; his own brand of cultural relativism extended to what was later called the "Sapir-Whorf hypothesis," i.e., the idea that linguistic categories structure culture.

Chapter 2

Margaret Mead Answers
(About the Future)

Margaret Mead is famously quoted as saying, "Never doubt that a small group of thoughtful, committed citizens can change the world." According to the Institute for Intercultural Studies (who holds the rights), hundreds of organizations have adopted this as their motto, embossing it on their letterheads or on placards in their boardrooms. Its popularity must be due, in no small part, to its ambiguity. What group? What change? What world? Applicable to neo-Nazis, environmentalists, liberals, conservatives, Mead's bon mots lend a vague optimism to any group's mission statement. The ambiguity, however, mirrors Mead's own ambivalences over culture change and the future and, in particular, gestures to her shift from directed, engineered change to one at once more profound but also more open-ended.

Why should we ask Mead about the future? No one anthropologist has said more about the things in life that interest people most, pace Gauguin's work, "d'ou venons nous ... que sommes nous ... ou allons nous." As Textor (2005: 11) has sagaciously noted, few anthropologists at the time loved the deictic "we" more than she did; if she were alive today, she would probably use Gauguin's painting on her homepage. But much of the critique of nineteenth century anthropology had been an excoriation of precisely the sorts of sweeping (and controversial) generalizations Mead loved to make. By the mid twentieth century, many anthropologists were uncomfortable making broad prognostications about the future of culture to the popular press, but that was Mead's element as a "public anthropologist." Moreover, tracing the course of her long career simultaneously sketches the problematic of the future of culture in anthropology from the perspective of someone who traversed, in her lifetime, three different epochs of anthropological thought.

And as globalization gave people the impression time was accelerating (à la Alvin Toffler's *Future Shock*), Mead's own ideas, as we shall see, seemed to accelerate toward some singularity that in many ways marked the emergence of something different entirely.

Contrary to the relativity implicit in anthropological theorizing on cultural development, anthropologists mostly labored under uniform conceptions of change; what was applied anthropology if not positively Newtonian? A force (an intervention, a development project, austerity measures) applied to some other "object" (a culture, a nation) produced change in a predictable direction. But was it this easy? What was to stop anthropologists from getting trapped in causal loops of their own devising? Like many Americans reading *Redbook* in the 1960s, we need only look to Margaret Mead for the answer. It was Mead who carried the chrono-cultural project from the nineteenth into the twentieth century.

Even more than Ruth Benedict and other Boasians, Margaret Mead retained an interest in E. B. Tylor's brand of cultural evolutionism; running like a subterranean river through her long, scholarly career, it is this evolutionism that provides the impetus for engineering culture change. From her very first published works *(Coming of Age in Samoa),* Mead reveals a desire to use ethnological data in order to inform engineered culture change in the West, famously recommending that parents in the US relax their sexual prudery in order to ease the pubescence of their children (di Leonardo 1998). We have to see this as very different than the kinds of social and political interventions from other Boasians that have weathered the test of time rather better than Mead's, such as the work and advocacy of St. Clair Drake, finally given credit after decades of racism-inflected obscurity (cf. Harrison and Harrison 1999). However, Mead's cultural tinkering was mostly submerged during her graduate years; it is only in the months leading up to the US involvement in World War II that Mead's proclivities toward the "reformer's science" reared up.

Mead's and Bateson's involvement in the "Committee on National Morale" led to an interest in utilizing anthropology to steer Allied cultures toward desired ends. In "Principle of Morale Building," Bateson and Mead (1941: 214) evoked this vision of anthropology through the "morale builder," who "is concerned with evoking, promoting resonance in, all those attitudes that are coherent and socially adaptive; and especially he is concerned with facilitating those changes in the group structure that may be necessary if the coherent character structure is to be maximally effective." Perhaps, as di Leonardo (1998) has suggested, because of her parent's work in business and advertising, Mead believed that culture was open to manipulation. And, despite the unproblematic (and almost automatic) process of acculturation that Mead's mentor, Ruth Benedict, described, Mead believed that culture—monolithic from the perspective of one submerged within it—was open to tinkering from without. Benedict (1934: 2–3) wrote that:

> The life-story of the individual is first and foremost an accommodation to the patterns and standards traditionally handed down in his community. From the moment of his birth the customs into which he was born shape his experiences and behaviors. From the time he can talk, he is a little creature of his culture, and by the time he is grown and able to take part in its activities, its habits are his habits, its beliefs his beliefs, its possibilities his possibilities.

By most accounts, this was a closed system, ultimately deterministic of a kind of modal personality. Mead's approach departed from this more mechanical model, and Mead was later to defend this aspect of Benedict's theory as being altogether more flexible than *Patterns of Culture* might indicate:

> We can contribute the practicality, the insistence that the job be done scientifically, on an engineering basis, insisting that we must know what the materials are—human beings of diverse cultures, human cultures of different designs, human societies of different constitution—out of which to build. (Mead 1942: 249)

But what to engineer? Along with her morale-boosting blueprints with Bateson, Mead produced plans to change the diet of Americans to more readily accept war-time rations *(The Problem of Changing Food Habits)*, to improve relations between Allies *(The American Troops and the British Community: An Examination of the Relationship Between American Troops and the British)*, et cetera.

This will-to-engineer continued into Mead's 1944 founding of the Institute for Intercultural Studies, which, while mostly concerned with national culture studies (for example, Mead's *Soviet Attitudes Towards Authority* 1951), contained the germ of culture critique and culture change. That is, the "despotic" Russian character might be ameliorated through interventions into swaddling (Gorer's "diaper" hypothesis), and all manner of undesirable, national traits (from the perspective of the anthropologists working in the United States) might be replaced with more modern, implicitly more American, characteristics:

> With such data, we can attempt to answer such questions as the following: What are the patterns of behavior between those in authority and those over whom they have authority? Are these patterns of behavior congruent with the ideals of behavior which are constantly preached in the schools and in the youth organizations? When we analyze the attempt to remake the old type of Great Russian into "the new Soviet Man" through adult education, political indoctrination,

> new forms of organization, and the attempt to bring up children to fit the ideals, do we find contradictions which may be sources of weakness in the present, or revolt, or of change in the future? (Mead 1955: 2)

And her wartime exegesis of American culture and personality, *And Keep Your Powder Dry* (1946), was, if not a masterpiece of writing (it was reportedly written in one week), a masterpiece of social engineering, lobbying, as Richard Handler (1990: 268) points out, "for social engineering to create a world organized in terms of the liberal, democratic values that Mead espoused." Here, Mead anticipated the Truman Doctrine by several years, arguing for an American *mission civilisatrice* that continues to haunt American foreign policy today, legitimating American hegemony abroad in a way that, perhaps, even the wartime Mead would not have approved. Nevertheless, to suggest that these were the forerunners of modernization theory in development (which continues today in the form of the free-market ideologies underlying the International Monetary Fund and the World Trade Organization) is not exaggerating. Mead, after all, helped found the Society for Applied Anthropology in 1941 and was its president in 1949.

After the War, Mead continued to pursue her interests in directed culture change, this time through her involvement (along with Gregory Bateson) in the Josiah Macy Jr. Conferences on Cybernetics, interdisciplinary congeries which met ten times over a period of seven years (1946–1953) to discuss the applications of Norbert Wiener's "cybernetics," "the field of control and communication theory, whether in machines or animals" (Wiener 1961: 11). Although Wiener had applied what would become information theory to physical systems (the nervous system, the homeostat, et cetera), Mead and Bateson wanted to apply it to cultural systems, using cybernetics to describe and predict deviance, schism, et cetera. This algorithmic approach to culture (anticipating later approaches to society by way of artificial intelligence modeling) was in many ways based on Mead's and Bateson's wartime prescriptions for culture change, conceptualized as hierarchies of leaders and followers, symbols and practice. But despite its consonance with cybernetics in physical systems, Wiener (24) expressed doubt that such a project might succeed and rather discouragingly confessed "I can share neither their feeling that this field has the first claim on my attention, nor their hopefulness that sufficient progress can be registered in this direction to have any appreciable therapeutic effect in the present diseases of society ... Thus the human sciences are very poor testing grounds for a new mathematical technique." Of course, Wiener's "cybernetics" proved to be much more than a mathematical technique modeling positive and negative feedback in a system; it became the sine qua non theory for the Cold War era, emphasizing, as N. Katherine Hayles (1999: 56–57) and others have pointed out, "equilibria and stasis." When Ashby's "homeostat" is applied to society, then all manner of perturbations (dissent, protest, heterogeneity, difference) become the enemy of the system and, like the progress of a ship or the temperature control in one's house, are subject to a "correction," which, when applied to politics, instantly takes on a sinister quality.[1]

Later, reflecting upon the transition of cybernetics to general systems, Mead applied cybernetics reflexively, suggesting that cybernetics acted as the basis for discussions as the philosopher's stone for overcoming cultural and linguistic barriers of all sorts:

> I had hoped, about ten years ago (and then advanced very briefly the idea) that we might be able to cross ideological boundaries which are on the whole, at present, the most important communications barriers in the world. We might be able to cross them by using cybernetics as a language, as value-free as physics, for physicists can meet and discuss a problem in physics, irrespective of the nations they belong to, or the military positions relating to their disagreement, as they exist at the time. (Mead 2005: 293)

The dream of this cybernetics has since been carried along by general systems and multi-agent systems, becoming both more complex (de-emphasizing equilibrium states) and altogether more stochastic. Eventually, as we shall see later, cybernetics would become the basis for the emergence of artificial life research and the sciences of complexity. But in the 1950s (and in many ways, today), it was an elitist model of change that counted "the people" only as epiphenomena of some feedback loop initiated further up the hierarchy of power and/or colonialism, an artifact of an altogether more technocratic age.[2]

The other critique of a cultural cybernetics, upon which countless anthropologists have elaborated, is that it, like the "culture and personality school," speciously represented other cultures as bounded entities, confusing (as US foreign policy makers do today) physical place with cultural practice (Collins 2004; Palumbo-Liu 2004). To be able to "regulate" feedback, one must, after all, identify the boundaries of the system, a task that has always involved some chicanery on the part of anthropologists. In fact, the sleight of hand that minimizes the impact of empire has been part of the arsenal of rhetoric that constitutes what Stocking called the "ethnographer's magic" (Collins 2007).

By the 1950s, the Macy Conferences had been canceled (which Mead always felt was premature), and Mead herself was moving on to other ideas of the future that diverged from those of the technocrat engineer she had become in the War years. For one thing, the United Nations had given her (and many of her contemporaries) hope that more universalist solidarities based on common languages, sciences, and governments might succeed national rivalries; for another, the nuclear arms race in the Cold War lent urgency to the universalist project. Mead, accordingly, began producing more effusive books and essays that waxed evocative and utopian rather than programmatic.

Also, as di Leonardo (1998) reports, Mead's work was falling out of favor with other anthropologists, the "culture and personality" school she was still best known for supplanted by more sophisticated (if not unassailable) theories, and her work during wartime unacknowledged by a professorate that was growing more politically active. Mead herself would come to acknowledge the shortcomings of "national culture studies." Speaking in retrospect, in 1975: "One reason that people dislike the study of national character is that it is skeletal. It is like grammar. If I described a language merely in terms of the grammar that we all share, it would be true, but it would not describe the range of vocabulary or sensitivity or our literary knowledge" (2005: 322) The underlying meaning, perhaps, is that "national culture" studies had a prescriptive air about them; that "modal" personality that made up the "skeletal" studies of the Institute for Intercultural Studies could just as easily be used to orientalize whole nations or, modus tollens, pathologize minority populations whose beliefs run counter to the "average." In addition, in the gradual thawing of McCarthyism and the recovery of anthropology from the wartime purges of progressives from universities and government, many anthropologists were eschewing involvement with government work that was looking more like empire building.

Mead, for whatever reason, was leaving behind simple algorithms of culture change and engineering for more open-ended systems and futures, following a general trend away from culture as discrete, bounded units. As Mead (2005: 312) recounted, "Variety has now been given a new standing it did not enjoy before. It is an answer to the people who advocated a unified world order, advocating the disappearance of all these idiosyncratic, odd little tribes and parochialisms in favor of uniformity and efficiency." The US and European baby booms, together with development of 1960s countercultures gave anthropology a huge boost in popularity and, with it, a more critical understanding of the kinds of unilinear modernization theory driving, for example, the establishment of ruinous "Indian schools" in the US. That said, Mead was not an uncritical proponent of imaginative evocations of the future. She felt that future possibilities were "handicapped" by the lack of imagination (1957: 958). And although her favorite novels were science fiction, she remained critical of the lack of imagination they displayed toward the future:

> It is significant how extremely difficult it has been for the prophetic writers of science fiction to imagine and accept an unknown future. At the close of *Child-*

hood's End, Arthur Clarke wrote: "The stars are not for men." ... Space operas picture the return of the last broken spaceship from imagined galactic societies to the "hall of beginnings" on Terra of Sol. In the *Midwich Cuckoos,* John Wyndham killed off the strange, golden-eyed, perceptive children bred by earth women to visitors from outer space. The film, *2001: A Space Odyssey,* ended in failure. This deep unwillingness to have children go far into the future suggests that the adult imagination, acting alone, remains fettered to the past. (1972: 47)

From the 1950s until her death, much of Mead's critical output moved from more programmatic pronouncements to more ludic evocations of cultures that may be, whether on this Earth or beyond.

The transitional text for this was her *New Lives for Old* (1956), a restudy of the Manus of the Admiralty Islands off the coast of Papua New Guinea that she had initially examined in *Growing Up in New Guinea* (1930). Her initial visit there in 1928 echoed the nineteenth century project of putting people in their correct temporality, and certainly would have been at home among Lévy-Bruhl, especially since she saw the work as more or less consonant with her museological mission at the American Museum of Natural History, where she was curator from 1926 to 1969: "As far as I myself was concerned, I wanted to work among some Melanesian people in order to enlarge my experience for the Museum and to study the way in which primitive adults, who were said to think like civilized children, differed from primitive children" (1956: x). Indeed, the work combines the universalism of the culture and personality school (gender, Freud, et cetera) with the theory of the unilinear evolutionist. *Growing Up in New Guinea* was not her most fondly remembered fieldwork, and she wrote later that when she left, she never thought to go there again: "taking with me all I needed to know of their strange and savage life" (xi).

However, Melanesians were not to be confined to their "primitive" life for long. During World War II, the US military moved millions of troops through Melanesia in the Pacific Theater, precipitating sweeping changes. Mead minimized the adverse impact of US troops, however, merely noting that "During the war, as a million of our troops poured through the Admiralty Islands, a mere thirteen thousand people were the audience, weighing the behavior of one American to another, building what they learned into a background for a new way of life" (1956: 9). By this curious euphemism, that the Manus were the "audience" for US troops, Mead implied that culture change would be a matter of mimesis rather than enforced. Indeed, the restudy of the Manus was to be an example of freely embraced, positive change: "This precious quality which Americans have developed, through three and a half centuries of beginning life, over and over, in a virgin land, is a belief that men can learn and change—quickly, happily, without violence, without madness, without coercion, and of their own free will" (6). More recent scholarship on "cargo cults" and such belies the racist notion of happy natives dreaming of Western consumer products (Kaplan 1995). But this model of embraced change, of "a people who have moved in fifty years from darkest savagery to the twentieth century, men who have skipped over thousands of years of history in just the last twenty-five years is offered as food for the imagination of Americans, whom the people of Manus so deeply admire" (Mead 1956: 6). That is, in a chronopolitical inversion that would not have been imaginable in Tylor's time, Mead's restudy of Manus was meant to act as a blueprint for rapid change elsewhere, including the US.

The book eventually settles on a charismatic movement similar to other "cargo cults" in Melanesia but, as Mead suggested, tied more to modernization than to the achievement of prosperity itself. Since what came to be known as the Paliau Movement (as well as the movement's leader, Paliau himself) welcomed rapid change and was able, in Mead's estimation, to accommodate that change without untoward stress or dislocation, Mead turned from using Manus as paradigmatic of the primitive (in 1930) to paradigmatic of the modern (in 1956):

> Thus it can be seen that throughout human history there has been a struggle between the proponents of closed and open systems, systems that could change their forms, accommodate new ideas, retain their allegiance of new generations within them rather than goad them into rebellion or desertion, systems that welcomed the ideas, the questions, and the members of other systems, and those contrasting elements which hardened into exclusiveness or conservativism, so that wars of contrast, the rack, the ritual trial, the war on unbelievers in which one attained merit by killing them, became their destructive method for self-perpetuation. (1956: 457)

Here, Mead alludes to her work with the Macy Foundation, but the "system" she advocates is in striking opposition to the closed systems that first generation of cybernetic thinkers were advocating.[3] And this book is concerned not so much with abstracted systems as charismatic individuals: Paliau, along with others, whom she identifies as "new men" or followers of the "New Way." *New Lives,* on the one hand, documents post-War processes of modernization; on the other, it is the drama of how these men (and it is always men) were or were not able to reinvent their lives in a world of American Empire as well as convince others to do the same under their leadership. John Killipak, for example, plays just such an ambivalent role. Mead cites, approvingly, his curiosity for the foreign, his desire for the "New Way," and his confident leadership, but also notes that,

He was simply a man who got caught short by the very rapid changes. Where the New Way had offered to Raphael Manuwai and Michael Nauma the same type of roles they would have played in the old society, had given Banyalo and Karol Manoi new roles which would not have been available to them—as cultural expatriate and immigrant with shallow ties—Killipak was caught between two worlds. (392–393)

The heroes of *New Lives* are precisely those people who are best able to embrace the fluid social structures characteristic of rapid change. Killipak, of course, had the last laugh on the question of the cosmopolitan, opening an exhibition of photographs of Mead's fieldwork at the University of Pennsylvania in 1979 and, in the process, suggesting a nice inversion of her objectifying gaze (Dillon 1980: 320).

But this question of the power of some individuals to anticipate and capitalize on what anthropologists would later characterize as the forces of globalization interested Mead; it was a topic she would take up in her largest theoretical work, *Continuities in Cultural Evolution* (1964), also her last effort to really enjoin anthropological colleagues.

Starting from a lecture she'd delivered at Yale University in 1957, *Continuities* elaborates a new theory of evolution—"microevolution"—that, Mead hoped, might mediate between the sort of historical particularism of the Boasians and the evolutionary studies then staging a renaissance in the work of Julian Steward, Leslie White, Elman Service and Marshall Sahlins, Walter Goldschmidt, et cetera:

> So, the rhythmic relationship has continued, creating a climate of opinion in which a threefold approach to evolution can now flourish: studies of evolution that deal with very long time periods and with enormous changes that accompanied man's cultural developments after the appearance of Homo sapiens; studies of comparable evolutionary sequences, in which human groups, starting with a common stock of ideas, have worked them out in comparable ways (Steward's multilinear evolution); and studies of processual change as they occur in one generation or between adjacent generations. (1964: 22–23)

"Microevolution" dealt with pivotal movements, localizable instances, when the work of individuals and small groups could be isolated as the cusp at which more abstract evolutionary change took place. She defines just such an "evolutionary cluster" as "an intercommunicating group of human beings who stand at some crucial point of divergence in a process of culture change." In other words, Mead is building a ladder from history (for example, the life history of individuals) to evolution (the development of large-scale stages of human development). And in the process reasserting her own relevance to anthropological theory as well as, importantly, building a bridge from her "applied" work to more "academic" theorizing.

Accordingly, she begins with what she believes to be just such pivotal moments: the US Congress debates on the metric system (as an example of the growth of democratic evolution) and the Paliau Movement (the growth of modernization). Yet, reviewers found the examples lacking. Why would these count as instances of "microevolution"? What "crucial point" did these represent? Did no one in the US ever stage a debate before then? Why would this charismatic cult be more pivotal than other events in Melanesia's tumultuous modernization? And how do we move from one "level" to the next (individual, specific, general)? As a theory of evolution, Mead's book left much to be desired, as reviewers (see Frantz 1966; Haydu 1966) pointed out.

As the book moves along, though, the focus of the argument shifts, from building a "unified field theory" of evolution to attempting to engineer situations that might prove of evolutionary significance. It's almost as if Mead has forgotten (or abandoned) her synthetic pretensions for something else entirely, relating less to theory in anthropology than to her own interests in small group dynamics and her own status as a public intellectual. That is, from building an explanatory body of theory describing events in the past to advocating (à la the reformer's science) for the kinds of creative situations in which new ideas and change might flourish:

> A formula distilled from these experiences would come to something like this: A conference would provide a guaranteed opportunity to meet some vividly first-class people in a noncompetitive and intense atmosphere. The conversation would come to an end and be resumed. There would be freedom to talk and freedom to listen, and the web of meaning would be woven as we talked, making a new pattern before our eyes. ... For such an emergent cluster no precise formula can be written. The only possible formulation is a delimitation of the conditions under which clusters of this kind can come into being. (1964: 301)

It's unclear, though, how this "emergent cluster" relates to the "clusters" she introduces in the first part of the book (for example, the Paliau Movement) and what becomes obvious after a while is that she has moved from evolutionary theory to creativity: How can you engineer the production of the conditions under which creative, interdisciplinary ideas can be generated? The best examples, it seems, are drawn from her own life. Even *Continuities* itself is said to emerge from just such a perspicacious meeting of minds:

> Two pieces of writing, *Male and Female*, written in 1948, and *Cultural Determinants of Sexual Behavior*, first written in 1950 for the compendium, *Sex and Internal Secretions*, which I was able to discuss extensively with Evelyn Hutchinson, focused

my attention on the need to integrate more specifically our knowledge of man's species-characteristic behavior, the peculiarities introduced by domestication and our knowledge of cultural evolution. An invitation to participate in the second of two Symposia on Behavior and Evolution, organized by Anne Roe and George Simpson in 1955 created the necessary focus. I found then that I had to go back over the whole question of appropriate units of cultural evolution to the inquiries begun in organizing *Cooperation and Competition Among Primitive Peoples,* to *Naven,* and to discussions with Gregory Bateson, Lawrence K. Frank and J.H. Woodger in the summer of 1939, and to the attempt to find a unit for the study of cultural patterns of nutrition. (xxv–xxvi)

Indeed, Mary Catherine Bateson makes the point that Mead's life is best understood anthropologically and that, in many ways, Mead anticipates the reflexive turn in the 1980s (1984: 272). It is not hyperbole to suggest that Mead was one of the first postmodernists in anthropology, although she (as a proud member of the AAAS) would have almost certainly objected to such a cognomen.[4]

In the above account, the cascading chain of meetings leads Mead to reevaluate both her earlier work and earlier meetings; her ideas emerging in the frisson of just such creative clusters. For her, the most valuable experiences—the most fecund moments—were those spent at institutes and workshops with interdisciplinary teams of scholars. This was the strength of the Macy conferences, which were, for some participants, merely chaotic. But, again, this was not something that one could unproblematically engineer. Her discussion of her experiences at the Menniger Foundation suggests this inchoate, almost hermetic quality:

A cluster of institutions like the Menniger Foundation and its associates in Topeka, Kansas, comes close to the setting in which new ideas come easily. Here, in a city which is also the state capital, are two large private clinics, one for adults and one for children, to which come the privileged and the rich. Here also are a great veteran's hospital, a state hospital, a state treatment center for children, an industrial school for boys, and a rehabilitation center for the blind.... The city is large enough so that it is not a mere appendage of the institutions in and around it, and it is small enough so that people meet frequently in different combinations. (1964: 304–305)

Given this laundry list of institutions common to any mid-sized city, it is unclear what transformations would result in a Menniger Foundation in Topeka, but not one in, say, Austin. But this is not a casuistry for evolutionary clusters, which, for Mead, retain epigenetic properties, which, of course, moves counter to the first part of the book altogether. That is, Mead moves from theory to an open-ended cosmopolitanism, from stressing the integration of culture as her friend and mentor Ruth Benedict did to something more along the lines of Richard Sennett.[5]

Of course, in many ways Mead would seem like an unlikely apical ancestor for anthropology's encounter with the cosmopolitan. Her work in Samoa, New Guinea, and Bali, become, for her, "natural laboratories" where cultural proofs could be constructed out of reified, anthropological "types." As di Leonardo (1998) and others have pointed out, she militantly ignored the ruinous colonialism invading Samoa and the Admiralties during her fieldwork; her's might be understood as some of the most "billiard ball" studies produced in the "culture and personality" school she helped create. Whatever other directions her research subsequently took, she rested much of her legitimacy as an anthropologist on her authoritative pronouncements on these people and the way they fit into the "savage-slot," that is, as indicia of "natural" prevalences in humanity that could be compared with their "civilized" counterparts in various, critical ways (Trouillot 1991).

However, even though her anthropological reputation was built on these stentorian pronouncements on the primitive, has there ever been a more cosmopolitan anthropologist? Not only did she live in New York for the entirety of her adult life, but she was also a globetrotter without peer. Reading her correspondence filed away at the Library of Congress is to experience travel envy. As she wrote to Wilton Dillon in 1961: "After the WFMH Roffey Park meeting, I came back to NY for six weeks, worked furiously on the ubiquitous Terry Lectures, then back to three delightful weeks in Paris, three days in Athens making a speech, and twelve days traveling around Sicily with Geoffrey, thinking about a reorganization of European studies of cultural depth, including surviving peasant societies" (Margaret Mead papers, correspondence). But her resolutely urban life did not follow the perambulations of Walter Benjamin or Charles Baudelaire, nor did her life correspond to the types identified by Georg Simmel. Missing from her letters is that sense of what Freud calls the *unheimlich*, the uncanny, those mind-bending experiences of radical alterity that found their way into Baudelaire, Poe, and that first generation of sociologist flâneurs. Mead's early life in New York was characterized by a certain amount of flâneurie: trips on the bus and subway with Ruth Benedict after class, poetry readings all over the city that included other anthropologist poets like Edward Sapir, et cetera. But as her fame grew, these sorts of urban adventures became less tenable. And her encounters with people became highly choreographed affairs meticulously arranged through her support staff back at the Museum; appointments were made months in advance, and she was a consummate multitasker before the term took on its current, clichéd weight:

The thing she was still most afraid of in the world, Mead said at the AAAS party, was being bored. She had long ago determined to take charge of every hour of her life: "Empty time stretches forever. I can't bear it." Rather than ride alone in a cab to La Guardia Airport, she was driven by her student Mary Elder, who brought along a videotape machine Mead could hold in her lap to see the work Elder had been doing with midwifery. With other young colleagues she made breakfast dates for five o'clock in the morning. Only once did Jean Houston make the mistake of inviting Mead to the theater. She had loved going to plays in earlier years, but now she had less and less taste and time for Broadway, and even less, Houston thought for small talk or girl talk. (Howard 1990: 392–393)

This style of life meant not only a very full life, as anyone knows who has perused Mead's schedules at the Library of Congress (LC), but also a (then) novel way of working, a form of scholarship positioned at the node of interlocking, complex networks. For Mary Catherine Bateson, the seamless multitasking, the vast network, was synecdochically encapsulated in the notebook Mead carried everywhere:

The notebooks stand in my mind for a whole way of working whereby she was constantly taking in new material and using it, so that an interesting piece of work she was thinking or writing in Boston, elaborated in Cincinnati, incorporated in a lecture in California. She tried to be conscientious about giving credit and would often put people working on related matters in touch with each other, but no amount of care for references to formal pieces of work could sufficiently reflect the extent to which all her speeches represented a legion of voices. John Todd, the ecologist, has designed a ship to be named for her, built as a wind-driven ecological hope ship that will move around the world providing various kinds of ecological first aid. Picking up seeds and seedlings of rare plants, particularly food plants, and propagating and growing them at sea so that they can be ready to plant or introduce as new crops on arrival in the next port, and this is what she did with ideas. (1984: 67)

This was Mead's model of invention, derived from her own autobiography. That is, ideas emerge in an unexpected way when creative people get together (it's hard not to see the influence of this on that "creative class" idea, or, for that matter, a whole generation of dot.com venture capitalists) (Ross 2004).

This is the preoccupation with her *Culture and Commitment* (1970), a nonacademic essay directed at Mead's many, popular audiences, and especially younger peoples, with whom she felt she had an especially strong connection (although we don't know how much of that was reciprocated by her students). In that essay, the "younger generation" and the counterculture are the protagonists, dragging their elders into the future in a rapidly changing world that Mead felt the pre-World War II generation was particularly unqualified to understand: "Instead of the erect, white-haired elder who, in postfigurative cultures, stood for the past and the future in all their grandeur and continuity, the unborn child, already conceived but still in the womb, must become a symbol of what life will be like" (83). Mead refused to predict the future, here, insisting that "we must now move towards the creation of open systems that focus on the future—and so on to children, whose capacities are least known and whose choices must be left open" (87).

This was plainly evident in one of her often-delivered speeches, one that was eventually known as "Our Open-Ended Future":

> Just twenty years ago, in the 1950's, we believed that one day spaceships would be able to move us out to colonize other planets in our solar system. In this belief, people did not worry about exhausting our planet's resources and the booming population; they perpetuated a very exploitative economy which is at the root of our most serious problems today.
>
> We know now, thanks to more recent scientific advances, that we are alone in this solar system of ours; there is no place in it for us but this small and very vulnerable planet we call Earth, and nobody on this earth but "Homo sap," such as he is. That is all we've got. For the first time in human history, we are aware of our responsibility to protect the earth and all life that lives upon it. This awareness has already significantly altered our vision of future alternatives—just as further knowledge (i.e., the discovery of other intelligent civilizations in the galaxy and communication with them) will give us a different perspective on man's place in the universe and make our current notions of the future obsolete. (2005: 330)

Our vision of the future of culture would be supplanted by other visions—our prognostications would prove short sighted, a product of our time. Jameson has said the same of utopia, that its role is to gesture beyond present imagination, hemmed in by the "prison-house" of language that ensures that we affirm the status quo even in the act of critiquing it.

NOTES

1. This was one of the more damning critiques of functionalism as a theory and went to the heart of anthropology's wartime involvement with government and propaganda (cf. Gregg and Williams 1948).
2. That is, Mead took the idea of an integrated "culture pattern" and, like proponents of structural functionalism, applied a thermodynamic model tinctured

with Benedict's libidinal economy to social and culture change—i.e., pressure applied in one area of culture affects change in another.

3. See Hayles (1999) for her useful periodization of cybernetic theorizing over the last fifty years.

4. Taking cues from autobiography and literary theory, many anthropologists in the 1980s tried to "insert themselves" in their ethnographic narratives. Although these experiments occasionally devolved into bathetic narcissism, they were nevertheless an improvement over "scientific" narratives that concealed the intersubjectivity of fieldwork under a third-person, "objective" patina.

5. Sennett, along with Jane Jacobs, can be credited with introducing the value of disorder into urban planning (1990).

Chapter 3

Chad Oliver:
An Anthropologist on *Star Trek*

Nineteenth-century utopian writings and "lost race" sagas notwithstanding, anthropological science fiction is generally thought to be a twentieth-century phenomena associated with John W. Campbell's editorship of what became *Astounding Science Fiction.*[1] Included in this sixty-year elaboration of what Raymond Williams has called "space anthropology" are a range of diverse writers, including Michael Bishop, Ursula K. Le Guin, Chad Oliver, Joanna Russ, and Ian Watson and (Clute and Nicholls 1995). Oliver is in many ways the exception: an anthropologist at the University of Texas, Oliver (1928–1993) worked in both fields, producing anthropological science fiction like *Unearthly Neighbors* (1984a) and *The Shores of Another Sea* (1984b) alongside academic writings like *Ecology and Cultural Continuity as Contributing Factors in the Social Organization of the Plains Indians* (1962), and a textbook introduction to anthropology, *The Discovery of Humanity* (1981). And, although he superficially tried to separate them, signing "Symmes C. Oliver" to his anthropology and "Chad Oliver" to his science fiction until the 1970s, Oliver saw them as productively interrelated enterprises: "I like to think that there are compensations, that there's a kind of feedback, an ideal fantasy, that the kind of open-minded perspective in science fiction conceivably has made me a better anthropologist. And on the other side of the coin, the kind of rigor that anthropology has, conceivably has made me a better science fiction writer" (quoted in 1984, Peterson). He even wrote a Guggenheim application for a grant to write a novel in accordance with anthropological theory (Chad Oliver Collection: Box 17[50]).[2] Indeed, his whole career can be seen as a struggle to mediate between his twin vocations. His fictions, I argue, should be understood in the context of that tension between anthropology and SF.

However, anthropology and science fiction changed a great deal during the space of Oliver's career and his work both reflects and anticipates those changes. The following chapter attempts to illustrate ways in which Oliver's work both reflects the anthropology and science fiction of his time, while at the same time, through his bifurcated perspective as both academic and writer, challenging some of the conventions in each. Indeed, this approach to his oeuvre would seem consonant with what Oliver himself was thinking in a 1974 American Anthropological Association paper: "When I was first exposed to anthropology, as an undergraduate, I experienced an immediate sense of familiarity; I felt that I was in the same universe of discourse. The problems of culture contact and culture conflict, the discussions of cultural relativism, the idea of cultural evolution, the whole emphasis on looking at things from different perspectives, the questions about what it meant to be human—all of these were as characteristic of science fiction as they were of anthropology" (1974a: 6). But this is not to reduce anthropology to its "fictions" (to paraphrase the interpretive anthropologist Clifford Geertz), nor to suggest that science fiction necessarily incorporates anthropology, but to gesture to the larger contexts of which both anthropology and science fiction form a part.[3] Following upon Marilyn Strathern's insight that "culture consists in the way people draw analogies between different domains of their worlds" (1992: 47), the very existence of "anthropological science fiction" as a critical term is in itself significant in that each presupposes what anthropology is while at the same time suggesting an affinity between these two projects.

Oliver's importance lies not with some ultimately fatuous concatenation of anthropology and science fiction, but with his strategic deployment of one to develop, critique, and imagine the other. In this way, we might see Oliver as the critical foil for Mead. Starting from similar places as social scientists ready to apply anthropology in order to tweak the cultural problems of the day, Oliver is at once more ludic (writing science fiction where Mead dealt in fact) and more critical (using fiction to explore the limits of, for example, some of the excesses of post-War social engineering), Oliver fills in the gaps of Mead's future visions and, together with Mead, sets the stage for more contemporary imaginings of cultural futures. The final portion of the chapter will, therefore, explore the legacy of Oliver's work for, on the one hand, an anthropology very much imbricated in the future and, on the other, a science fiction that (in the work of writers like Octavia Butler and China Miéville) has again begun to parallel and anticipate developments in anthropological thought.

As a child, Oliver's exposure to science fiction came from pulp magazines, including *Astounding Science-Fiction* and *Amazing Stories.* He began writing during a protracted, childhood illness when he penned long letters to their editors. His first story was "The Imperfect Machine," published in the *Texas Literary Quarterly* in 1948. And even though it precedes his interests in anthropology, it nevertheless sets the tone for his later work. John Thornton is to be the first man in space. His ship—the Stellar Queen—works perfectly. The "imperfect machine" is, of course, John Thornton himself, who, unprepared for extraplanetary travel, deteriorates into Lovecraft-ian babbling: "He was alone. Alone as no human being had ever been alone before. Alone and small, small! Little and alone and afraid. He was utterly, absolutely insignificant. Millions upon millions of stars swam out there in the sea of space, more than he could ever see, more than he could imagine. They mocked his tiny dreams.... It was vast. It was huge. It was beyond comprehension. It was shattering his mind, and he could not look away. Could not, could not, could not" (23). While certainly sophomoric (and written while Oliver was a college sophomore), John Thornton's travails prefigure the anthropocentrism of Oliver's mature fiction; machines may be invented that may enable all sorts of heretofore unimaginable things, but the central problem will always be people themselves.

Oliver graduated from the University of Texas with a BA in English literature and went on for a Masters in English, writing his thesis on science fiction ("They Builded a Tower"). However, at some point in the midst of his graduate education, he realized that his true interests were in anthropology, and in 1952 he was accepted to UCLA's doctoral program in anthropology under Walter Goldschmidt. In Los Angeles, steeped in anthropology and surrounded by a writers like Charles Beaumont, Richard Matheson, and William Nolan (retrospectively referred to as "the group"), Oliver entered into the most prolific period in his writing career.

Matheson's and Beaumont's penchants for Cold War paranoia and surprise endings—so notable in Matheson's *I Am Legend* (1954) and Beaumont's scripts for "The Twilight Zone"—soon became staples of Oliver's writing. Indeed, he produced several stories that had a "Twilight Zone" feel to them (what Clute and Nicholls describe as "sting-in-the-tail plotting" [1995: 1249]) and may have even sold scripts to the series. In "Technical Advisor" (1953), a science fiction writer—Gilbert Webster—is hired to advise a director—Dee Newton—for an SF movie. For the sake the verisimilitude, Newton flies them all out to the Moon, whereupon Webster discovers that it's the Martians who are making the movie about humans. The consummate opportunist, Webster hires on as technical advisor for the Martian's movie: "Webster smiled back—and found that he was able to move again. He flexed his stiff muscles and actually felt happier than he had been in years. Technical advisor for a Martian film company, working with a real scientist like Newton! What if he was a Martian—Webster wasn't prejudiced" (40). While certainly less dark than Matheson and less urbane than Beaumont, Oliver's writing shared their direct writing style. And although Oliver later cited Heinlein as a major influence, his writing would bear the imprint of "the group" for the remainder of his career.

Early on, his letter and fiction writing attracted the epistolary attentions of John W. Campbell (to whom Oliver sold at least seven stories) who used Oliver, as he did many of his writers, as a sounding board for his sociological and anthropological theories, exhorting them to write stories in accordance with his extraordinarily fecund, if hackneyed and right-wing, ideas about civilization, history and culture.[4] Campbell's letters to Oliver were similar to ones sent Isaac Asimov, James Blish, and Robert Heinlein: dense, encyclopedic montages of pop-intellectualism designed, seemingly, to both instruct and infuriate: "Chad, studying ancient civilization is not going to lead directly to answers for modern civilization, unless they learn enough to devise a Linnean classification system for cultures. A culture is very much like a living organism, with individuals acting in the role of cells. So far, we haven't got any very high-order social organisms; to date, our highest, the Western, seems to me on the order of a hydra" (COC: 10/24/52, Box 1[30]). Characteristically, Campbell is blissfully unaware of the vast anthropological literature on this very subject (although the civilization-as-hydra metaphor seems to be an original, Campbell contribution). Nevertheless, Oliver takes Campbell quite seriously, patiently outlining the anthropological theories he was learning at UCLA to Campbell and writing several stories as rejoinders to Campbell's ideas. In a 1952 letter, he even assigns Campbell some homework:

> In re your current (February) editorial, I wonder if some of the anthropological work might not throw some light on the problem. It may be that we have a dichotomy of sorts on our hands here; is "thinking" one distinct operation, done with one organ, or is it an interacting, functional process of the whole organism? In any event, *what* people think—as opposed to *how* they do it—is unquestionably determined to a vast extent by the elusive clutter known as culture, spelled environment by the sociologists. For an interesting discussion, try Dr Leslie White's *The Science of Culture,* in particular chapters IV ("Mind is Minding") and VII ("Cultural Determinants of Mind"). (Chapdelaine, second reel)

Indeed, it was this dialogue that framed much of Oliver's writing in the 1950s—both in SF and in anthropology.

As we saw in chapter 1, it would be a mistake to say that cultural evolutionism disappeared in the early twentieth century. Even as Spencerian schemes were formally vilified, critics like Marshall Hyatt and George Stocking show that emphases on culture change together with a comparativist undercurrent preserved the ultimately Spencerian idea that cultures "evolve" toward formations of greater and greater complexity and, moreover, can be sorted according to characteristic "types." As Robert L. Carneiro (2003) cheerfully observes, even the most stalwart of critics nevertheless held to popular understandings that rated, for example, state societies as more "advanced" than other political forms. After all, even Boas's students (for example, Alfred Kroeber and Clark Wissler) had always preserved the spirit (as well as the typologies) of nineteenth century evolutionist thinkers like Lewis Henry Morgan.

It was this agglutinative approach that Chad Oliver learned, first as an undergraduate with J. Gilbert McAllister and, later, as a doctoral student with Walter Goldschmidt, who had been Alfred Kroeber's graduate student at the University of California, Berkeley, and, therefore, heir to Kroeber's blend of Boasian particularism and nineteenth century generalization. Combining a technocratic faith in the powers of science to improve human life with more liberal belief in self-determination borne of cultural relativism, this anthropology exuded confidence for the future. As Oliver (COC: 2/4/53, Box 1[70]) explained to Campbell,

> We do not, of course, have all of the answers. I don't know what the "ultimate" solution will be, but I am confident of this: if there are solutions, they will incorporate the data of anthropology—which is, after all, an integrating science in itself.
>
> The social scientists will develop, and have already to an extent developed, necessary preconditions and associated facts that go within a given complex. That is to say, they will be able to predict in a general way what the results of a given technological innovation will be, what psychological stresses will accompany a given social structure, what the individual can and cannot do in a given environment, what steps may be taken to neutralize a specific trouble situation in a functioning culture, and the like.

That is, however idiosyncratic Campbell's pet theories might be ("civilization-as-hydra"), they were echoes of an anthropology with one foot in the nineteenth century now firmly chained to post-War ideologies of scientific progress and to the achievement of a better society through techno-rational planning. And it was this anthropology, so readily evident in Goldschmidt's *Man's Way* (1959), that formed the basis of Oliver's graduate education at UCLA.

Not surprisingly, Oliver's science fiction from this period is inflected with this propensity for social engineering.[5] In "The Ant and the Eye" (1971), anthropologists use their expertise in manipulating cultural variables to save the planet from destruction. By controlling certain social factors—in this case preventing Donald Weston from being elected to public office in Galveston, Texas—these "cultural tinkers" could stave off positive feedback in the cybernetic system. And in "Field Expedient" (1971), anthropologist Keith Ortega engineers new "culture patterns" on Venus in order to vouch-safe human creativity threatened in an increasingly stagnant Earth culture.

> The early socioculturists had made a science out of the primitive social disci-plines of psychology, sociology, anthropology, and economics. The Venus colo-nies were products of that science.
> One thing about a science: it works.
> If an engineer knows his business, his bridge does not fall down.
> If a socioculturist knows *his* business, his culture does what he wants it to.
> (153)

Other stories—for example, "Mother of Necessity" (1955a) and "Night" (1955b)—can be seen as similarly confident predictions of a mature anthro-pology that, through the discovery of universal, ineluctable laws of cultural development, can be used to direct culture change.

This reaches a crescendo with *Shadows in the Sun* (1954) and *The Winds of Time* (1957), novels which would for many define Oliver's oeuvre. In *Shad-ows*, Paul Ellery is an anthropologist who bears an uncanny resemblance to Oliver himself—tall (Oliver was 6´3″), always smoking a pipe, and enjoying a steak and a shot or two of whiskey. Inspired by W. Lloyd Warner's *Yankee City* and Hortense Powdermaker's *After Freedom,* he goes off to do a com-munity study of Jefferson Springs, Texas. At first, no one will talk to him. Later, "they had talked willingly and volubly. They had told him everything. Unfortunately, hardly a word of what they said rang true" (10). That is, Jef-ferson Spring turns out to be too typical, too normal.

> But, somehow, it didn't fit together as a coherent whole—or more precisely, it fitted together *too* well. The neighborhood maps, the statistics, the symbol sys-tems, the values—they added up to a perfect, ideal "type" that simply could not exist in reality. Social science was one devil of long way from being that precise in its predictions. No one had ever found an ideal "folk" society as conceptual-ized by Redfield, and no one could expect to find a community as typical in every way as Jefferson Springs.
> Still, he had found one. There were no ragged edges, no individual pecu-liarities, no human unpredictability.
> It was, in a word, faked data. (24)

As it turns out, the people of Jefferson Springs are all transplanted aliens. But those aliens, far from the Cod War monsters in movies like *The Thing* (1951), are normal folk, indistinguishable from denizens of 1950s America.

"It was man—another race of man, perhaps, but man for all that—writing the old, old stories on new paper with new machines" (37).

That is, these aliens are comprehensible in anthropological terms and, as such, it is anthropology, rather than the physical sciences, that promises a solution to the problem of alien colonization. According to the burgeoning science of anthropology, every society—no matter at what level of development—had to functionally meet certain human needs. "They had learned, long ago, that it was the cultural core that counted—the deep and underlying spirit and belief and knowledge, the tone and essence of living. Once you had that, the rest was window dressing. Not only that, but the rest, the cultural superstructure, *was relatively equal in all societies*" (1965: 115). For Ellery, the insight that the aliens are not "supermen" (a favorite Campbell-ian conceit) means that they are, despite their fantastic technologies, ordinary people with the expected array of weaknesses—laziness, factionalism, arrogance—whose cultural life is as predictable as any Earth society's. Not being superior means that they can be defeated and that the key to this lays not in the procurement of superior technologies, but in the creative cultural work of Earth people themselves.

In *The Winds of Time,* a spaceship from Lortas lands on Earth during Paleolithic times. The crew, complete with an anthropologist, priest, novelist, and dilettante, are, despite their interstellar origin, remarkably human. Their ship is one of several sent to explore the galaxy for inhabited worlds. The problem, however, is that the planets heretofore discovered evidence striking evolutionary convergence.

> The ships had discovered three kinds of planets that had developed men. On one type the men had not yet advanced to a state of technological development that gave them a chance to destroy themselves. On a second type, above the primitive level but not yet to the level of space flight, men were organized into groups, busily hacking away at each other with whatever weapons they could muster. On these worlds the Lortas were received with suspicion, with hostility, with fear. Their ships were impounded, their knowledge was used to fight in wars that were utterly meaningless to them. Crews that landed on these worlds seldom got home again.
>
> And there was a third type, of which Centaurus Four was a good example. On these worlds man had evolved, he had developed weapons powerful enough to do the job, and he was extinct. The methods varied: germs, crop bights, cobalt bombs, gas. The result was the same: extinction. (1957: 67)

Unable to fix their ship on a planet stuck in the first type, the Lortans settle in for several thousand years of hibernation, only to emerge in the United States in the 1950s. They manage to capture Weston Chase, who, in his capacities both as anthropological informant and audience for the story of their journey, manages to solve their problem by proposing another period of hibernation. The Lortans awake (with Chase at their side) in a future United States that has managed to survive into the next "stage" of evolution—global peace coupled with space travel.

Out of these two novels one might see both strains of Oliver's graduate education in dynamic tension: the cultural relativism of the inter-war years together with older, but still powerful, stagial theories of cultural evolution. In an afterward to the 1985 reissue of *Shadows in the Sun,* Oliver writes, "I was a graduate student at UCLA when I wrote this novel, working on a Ph.D. in anthropology. I was drenched in anthropology, as only a graduate student can be with his or her orals looming on the horizon. I believed in it, and more than that I felt that the insights of anthropology might well save this world of ours" (206). Indeed, similar to the battery of exams graduate students endure, Oliver attempts a synthesis of anthropology theory. It is the elaboration of this—and the tensions and even contradictions engendered in the process—that drive these stories. First, the problems that people might encounter in the far future will be eminently human problems, the solutions to which will lie in fuller understandings of people rather than in the adoption of advanced technology. As Paul Ellery's alien friend, John, explains, "they're just people. Take a jackass and give him an automobile, and he's still a jackass" (1954: 98). It is this strong, humanist strain that, perhaps, comes to define "anthropological science fiction." Heir to the cultural relativism of Ruth Benedict and Edward Sapir, the insistence that there is no such thing as a "primitive" mind or culture means that cultures must be understood on their own terms rather than as European antecedents. "Cultures"—whether on this planet or from other planets—are neither superior nor inferior; this insight has been of inestimable value in challenging the hegemony of technological development that underlies the social Darwinism latent in modernization theory.

The Winds of Time begins with the strident humanism of *Shadows in the Sun;* the Lortans are, for all their technology, all too human. To Weston Chase, their (involuntary) ethnographer, the Lortan's inexplicable "otherness" gradually gives way to rapport and empathy: "They were all so *different* from what they had seemed [...] The white-faced figure from hell that had chilled his blood that night so long ago was just Avron—a man with a different background from his own, but a man he understood for all that. So far as that went, he knew Avron better than the knew most of the people he saw every day in Los Angeles—and liked him better, too" (142). And yet, they are at the same time Chase's evolutionary "superiors"; the Lortans stand at the apex of a chain of unilinear development defined by space travel and military technologies. Weston Chase, as a representative of the United States, stands in as the highest level of evolutionary development for the Earth; the aliens have, in fact, been waiting for the development of the United States for thousands of years. In other words, to go back to Marshall Sahlins's influential 1960 essay, while "specific" evolution may be productive of a multiplicity of cultural possibilities, stagial theories of "general" evolution rank Western societies as the "most advanced."

Combining these two anthropological traditions, however, is, as anthropologists like Eric Wolf have amply demonstrated, detrimental to cultural relativism and, perhaps, ultimately, to Oliver's fiction. The aliens in *Shadows* and *Winds* are too familiar. Like the Earth people who become their interlocutors, the aliens value Western-style rationality, science and technology; their "alien" worlds seem little different than a United States with space travel and a strong United Nations. Quaffing their alien equivalents of whiskey, complaining about their alien equivalents of estranged wives, they are W. Lloyd Warner's "organization men" in polymer body suits and, while it may be useful to underline the familiar in the alien Other, Oliver's future seems drearily familiar. Why even bother if all we have to look forward to is Yankee City in space?

Perhaps the problem was that Oliver had never really left "Yankee City" to begin with. While he may have done some limited interviews with a Native American informant in Harlingen, Texas, it is significant that, until 1961, he does no extended, ethnographic fieldwork. Oliver's doctoral thesis—a library dissertation later published as *Ecology and Cultural Continuity as Contributing Factors in the Social Organization of the Plains Indians* (1962)—draws heavily on Walter Goldschmidt's theories in its analysis of the "horse-buffalo complex" as a common adaptation among Plains peoples to common material conditions. Manifest cultural differences between, say, Blackfoot and Cheyenne peoples, are consigned to "cultural survivals" that predate the arrival of the horse and the gun, and that had originated in significantly different ecologies—for example, horticultural production versus hunting and gathering subsistence (58). Oliver tries to organize a great deal of disparate information; in the end, it proves a productive, if labored, exercise (as dissertations are wont to be). Reading the work, one gets the feeling that Oliver is less engaged in studying Plains adaptations than with fitting the data into Goldschmidt's theories. That is to say, Oliver is not trying to understand the Crow, Comanche, or Cheyenne in themselves. Instead, the typological schema and the model of culture change are the ultimate object and the interpreting, synthesizing anthropologist the ultimate protagonist. His dissertation bears little resemblance to the "thick descriptions" of other cultures that came of age in the 1960s. However, his later research (and later fictions) would remedy this.

Nevertheless, this period, including Oliver's lively correspondence with John W. Campbell, his graduate school experience, and his association with "the group" in Los Angeles, marks the most productive period in his writing and publishing career. From the late 1950s, his duties as professor and, later, chair of the anthropology department at the University of Texas would limit the time he could devote to writing science fiction. In addition, his own more sober reassessment of anthropology's potential would temper his earlier stories of steak-and-whiskey-loving anthropologist-technocrats. He had, apparently, become tired of being cast as "the anthropologist who writes science fiction" in the wake of the popularity of *Shadows in the Sun*. According to an interview with Thomas Knowles in 1989, this is the reason he "kills off" the anthropologist (Deryyoc) early in *The Winds of Time*. Indeed, his movement away from the anthropologist-hero can be seen as part of an overall reappraisal of anthropology as a "scientific" discipline that could be used to engineer a better life. As he recounts in the 1985 reprinting of *Shadows in the Sun*, "It is somewhat disconcerting to see Paul Ellery turning again and again to his anthropological training, seeking answers that were not there" (206). Oliver's growing realization is that anthropology may not have all of the answers.

In *Unearthly Neighbors* (1984a), an anthropologist (Monte Stewart) is recruited to make "first contact" with aliens (the Merdosi) on a recently discovered planet. The Merdosi are humanoid in form but use no tools, build no homes, and wear no cloths; Monte and his team of anthropologists are convinced that the Merdosi are living in an abject, "primitive" state. This, however, leads to a series of tragic misunderstandings that culminates with the murder of Monte's wife and, after a period of soul searching and conversion, the beginnings of a tenuous reconciliation with the Merdosi.

> I'm convinced that the key to this whole thing is somehow mixed up with the fact that these people have no tools. We are so used to evaluating people in terms of the artifacts they use that we are lost when these material clues are denied to us. Making tools seems to us to be the very nature of man. The first things we see when we look at a culture are artifacts of some sort: cloths, weapons, boats, skyscrapers, glasses, watches, copters—the works. But most of this culture isn't visible. (105)

This insight leads him to discover the Merdosi's extraordinary mental powers, as "advanced" over those of the people in the United States as US technology is over that of the "primitive" Merdosi and, to a limited extent, share in their unfathomable mental life and therefore become accepted—in a truncated way—as a "person." This is a far cry from the near-omniscient, anthropologist-technocrats who populate Oliver's early work.[6]

From 1961–1962, Oliver accompanied Walter Goldschmidt and a team of anthropologists to East Africa (that is, Kenya, Uganda, and Tanzania) for research on the interrelationships of culture and ecology. Each of the researchers studied a different group of people, with the eventual goal of aggregating their results into a broader theory of cultural ecology. Oliver studied the Kamba of Kenya, splitting his time between primarily pastoral and primarily horticultural Kamba communities. His results ("Individuality, Freedom of Choice"), while confirming the general "fit" of cultural life and mode of production—the hallmark of Goldschmidt's cultural ecology— nevertheless demonstrate that culture resists easy explanation.[7] "To those who fall into the habit of thinking a culture as a kind of strait-jacket, the Kamba are an instructive lesson. The cloak of Kamba culture does in fact hang together with the appropriate functional stitching, but it is a voluminous and loose-fitting garment indeed" (1965c: 423). Oliver found his informants' individuality and pragmatic instrumentalism in some tension with Goldschmidt's non-agential ideas of cultures as epiphenomena of functional adaptations. This is by no means a challenge to Goldschmidt; he interprets several institutions—age grades, gender, circumcision ritual—in the context of ecological adaptation. Nevertheless, Oliver's work ("The Hills and the Plains") also demonstrates the limits of cultural ecology: "Finally, I do not suggest that cultural ecology (or any other theoretical approach now available) can 'explain' everything about a cultural system. Neither would I pretend that our experiences or predictions were confirmed in every instance by the Kamba" (1982: 156). Of course, long before anthropology's "reflexive turn" in the 1980s, anthropologists had long admitted that fieldwork—far from Malinowski's (1922) grand narratives of the anthropologist-hero in *Argonauts of the Western Pacific*—was messy, emotionally exhausting and deeply problematic.[8]

In the wake of this fieldwork and confronted by the ambiguities of real life, Oliver is altogether less sanguine of the ability of anthropology to solve social problems and direct cultural change.[9] As he confesses in a 1969 address to the University of Texas's "Town and Gown Club" (COC: Box 9[40]): "I remarked at the outset that I was going to offer a few unpopular opinions. I did not promise to offer any solutions. Indeed, one of my more unpopular opinions is the notion that there may not *be* 'ideal solutions' to all human problems. This goes against the grain of traditional American culture which holds that people are basically rational and that there are potential solutions to all problems if we all just work hard enough." This respect for the occasional incommensurability of life finds its way into Oliver's subsequent work and in particular his next science fiction novel, *The Shores of Another Sea* (1984b).[10]

In *Shores,* Royce Crawford (not an anthropologist) is in charge of a research center in Kenya when aliens land and take over the bodies of the baboons Crawford is studying. Much of the novel is enigmatic and unresolved, from the fractured, colonial setting to the inscrutable purposes of the aliens themselves who, never really able to "combine" with their baboon hosts, leave as enigmatically as they'd come.

> Royce did not know and could not guess where the great white sphere had come from, or where it had gone. He did not pretend to understand why the ship had come or what its inhabitants had sought. This small corner of alien earth had been a port of call, a mysterious island touched in the course of an alien Odyssey. Somewhere, perhaps, on a world lost in the depths of space, there was a Homer who would sing of the voyage, sing of Earth and the beings who lived there. (1984b: 204–205)

In many ways, the novel is very much unlike Oliver's preceding work; there is little moral resolution, nor is anthropology much help in determining what motivates the aliens. In striking contrast to the familiar chumminess of the alien in *Shadows in the Sun* and *The Winds of Time,* humans and aliens in *Shores* systematically misunderstand each other. In addition, there's much more of a sense in this novel of political reality. Kenya is portrayed as a postcolonial space riven with underdevelopment and inequality in a way very different from Oliver's published work on the Kamba where the colonial context was submerged in the process of presenting Kenya as a "natural laboratory" for the study of culture change and adaptation.[11] For Oliver, this more questioning attitude toward anthropological knowledge and the complicity of anthropology in the maintenance of colonialism were, perhaps, better expressed in fictions than in his academic work.

In fact, the intervening decade between Oliver's field research and the publication of *Unearthly Neighbors* (1984b) had been one of critical self-reflection in anthropology. In the United States, moral qualms about the Vietnam War together with evidence that anthropologists had been employed as spies and propagandists by the US government prompted critiques of anthropology's role in world systems of power. In development, various strains of dependency theory disrupted the self-congratulatory evolutionism of modernization theory with historical understandings grounded in political economy. Closer to home, Vine Deloria, Jr.'s *Custer Died For Your Sins* (1969) and civil rights groups like the American Indian Movement (AIM) skewered anthropology's paternalist pretensions. Two edited collections of essays—Dell Hyme's *Reinventing Anthropology* (1972) and Talal Asad's *Anthropology and the Colonial Encounter* (1973)—explored anthropology's colonial legacy and precipitated a critical engagement with ethics and the politics of representation.

In "Far From This Earth" (1974b), Oliver explores the neo-colonialism and dependency in recently independent Kenya. Stephen Nzau wa Kioko is a Kamba Senior Game Warden at "Safariland," a kind of East African Disneyland where, in the wake of "development," Africa has become so much commodified exotica to be consumed by jaded tourists.

> He showed his identification at the gate, trying not to look at the huge signs. He had to look at them, of course; that was the kind of signs they were. One read: SEE WILD AFRICAN ANIMALS IN THEIR NATURAL HABITAT! That wasn't bad, although many of the animals in the park were not really wild any longer and one could quibble about how natural the carefully managed habitat was. Another sign: SEE SAVAGE MASAI WARRIORS SPEAR A LION! The Masai weren't very savage these days, those that were left, and the sparring was a bloodless charade. … SEE MAU MAU FREEDOM FIGHTERS! Well, at least they were in the right country, although the Mau Mau in Safariland were a far cry from the ragged, desperate men Stephen had known—when? Long, so long ago. (205)

Through Stephen, Oliver explores a complex and unpleasant reality where the inequalities of the past continue into the present and the future offers few alternatives.[10]

Oliver seems to have endured his own period of questioning and critical self-refection. In fact, this period finds him at his most pessimistic, with little hope for the continued success of anthropology or, indeed, for the continued existence of Homo sapiens in general. In "The End of the Line" (1965a) and, particularly, in his dark, despairing story for Harlan Ellison's *Again, Dangerous Visions,* "King of the Hill" (1972), Oliver bemoans the "manswarm" that has polluted the countryside and overpopulated the cities; the only hope for redemption lies in those who might come after humans have killed themselves off. Given the strident optimism of his 1950s writings, it is almost incongruous that he would be included in Ellison's anthology of fashionably nihilistic, "New Wave" writers.

However, while anthropology may have offered him few, concrete solutions to the human problems of environmental degradation, overpopulation and war, Oliver nevertheless believed that anthropological insights might help humans to prosper in the future:

> Even if we assume that man is alone in this vast universe as a sentient or culture-bearing being—which I find at best a startlingly parochial hypothesis—or even if we assume that contact with others with whom we may share this immense universe of galaxy beyond galaxy is impossible for one reason or another—there is still a promise before us. It is the promise of cultural plurality. Even within

the constrictions of sophisticated technological constraints, there will be alternatives open to us.

And that, after all, is one of the messages of anthropology: that we are all human beings regardless of where we live or what we look like, that different solutions to the problems of living have value, and that in cultural diversity may be found the seeds of man's fulfilling whatever potentials he may possess. (1974a: 17)

That is, humans—human problems and human potentials—are still central for his vision of the future, but the important component of evolutionary thinking and social engineering has dropped away. That "general evolution" where, whatever the vicissitudes of the developments of specific cultures, the most "advanced" cultures (always the West with the occasional inclusion of Japan) represented the highest potential of human species being, makes room for the possibility of another kind of development. Oliver's insight that cultural plurality itself may enable the future amounts to nothing less than a critical, reinvention of cultural relativism.

In other words, the lifeways of other peoples are of more use than as mere "data" for a universalist theory of culture change. Instead, different cultures suggest different approaches to the human condition, potential sources of human creativity and strength that—whatever they may lack in "complexity" (à la Herbert Spencer) or "energy expenditure" (à la Leslie White)—may ensure the survival of the species. And this does not mean, as I have suggested, some sterile "archive" of cultural alternatives to be picked over by social scientists engineering the perfect society (Collins 2003). For example, in "The Gift" (Oliver 1974c), Lee Melner is given an opportunity to escape from the myopic, sealed city he inhabits in order to explore the world beyond: "Lee, there is another world out there, beyond the colony Dome. It is waiting for us. The air is good, the white sun shines, the strong winds blow. There are people out there. Not people like us, but they are humanoid. They have not forgotten how to laugh and how to dream. We have much to offer them. They have more to offer us" (43).[11] Instead of discovering aliens who are basically Earth technocrats in stage makeup, the value of the "Other" lies precisely in the challenge of radical alterity. That is, the process of cultural discovery is mutually beneficial and may prove salubrious to moribund, Western institutions. The chief impediment to this is the sort of dull uniformity where certain forms of organization replace heterogeneity with "rationalized" (but not rational) production and consumption, for example, in the opportunistic, global circulation of popular culture, McDonald's, and Walmart described in George Ritzer's work. Indeed, it is this premonition of global, cultural homogeneity that gives Oliver's 1960s and 1970s writings such a despairing tone; the hope for radical heterogeneity initiates a new period in Oliver's thinking.

And this marks a second turning point for Oliver's fiction as well. Writing against the uniformity of *Star Trek* futures, Oliver instead imagines the multiplication of cultural possibility. In "Ghost Town" (1983), the chance discovery of an isolated colony of hunters and gatherers in an "O'Neill" (a huge, self-contained space station named after the physicist Gerard O'Neill) gives Caroth, the dying patriarch, a chance to pass down his knowledge, culture, and superior mental powers to an archaeologist, Rick Malina.

In this fictionalized field setting, the anthropological project means both understanding cultural difference and this understanding's transformation of the anthropologist's own culture. That the future would be productive of heterogeneity is an important departure from an earlier era of cultural critique from anthropologists like Margaret Mead and Ruth Benedict that, despite its trenchant liberalism, as di Leonardo, Palumbo-Liu, and others have shown, contained a kernel of cultural conservatism (di Leonardo 1998; Palumbo-Liu 2002). For them, as for the earlier Oliver, cultures, grasped in isolation (qua national character studies), could be compared to one another, in the process transplanting particularly desirous institutions while at the same time clarifying central characteristics. And yet, these characterizations assumed both intracultural homogeneity and intercultural separation, both theses as untenable today (with globalization) as they were at most times in the past (Wolf 1982). The Other in these schemas appears as primitive caricature, *tableau vivant* episodes in the development of the West: "Here's what we looked like before industrialization."

In his post-1970s writings, Oliver is instead suggesting an actual transformation of the historically unequal relations that have (over)determined encounters between "West" and "rest," anthropological or otherwise. That moment of surrender, Oliver seems to be saying in his post-1960s work, is key to the survival of all human cultures; the moral of these stories is not to anthropologically theorize and (therefore) dominate as it is to allow the anthropological encounter to change the self. These evocations are, however, very different from the nostalgic longing for a "primitive" past, the simplistic utopias in which other peoples of the world have oftentimes been slotted at the very moment of their destruction at the hands of Western imperialism. And it would not be an exaggeration to suggest that Oliver's deployment of cultural relativism anticipates some of the interest in "heterotopias" and "alternative modernities" in anthropology, cultural studies, and cultural geography in the 1990s. As Arturo Escobar writes in *Encountering Development:* "At the bottom of the investigation of alternatives lies the sheer fact of cultural difference. Cultural differences embody—for better or for worse, this is relevant to the politics of research and intervention—possibilities for transforming the politics of representation, that is, for transforming social life itself. Out of hybrid or minority cultural situations might emerge other ways of building economies, of dealing with basic needs, of coming together into social groups" (1995: 225). Both Oliver and Escobar struggle to imagine an anthropology that, while abnegating a privileged access to truth, can nevertheless serve as a conduit or medium for cultural alternatives. The image of Caroth, the dying patriarch of the O'Neill, taking over the mind of Rick Malina is a particularly appropriate one; the opposite of cultural "others" conceived as so many "natural laboratories" for a universalist science of anthropology may be these strategic moments of submission, when dominant knowledge is overturned—if only for a moment—by alternative epistemologies. This is very different than a cultural engineering that would presuppose the direction of change and the omniscient knowledge of the cultural Other; this seems more subversive of institutionalized knowledge practices. Through such a critical anthropology lies the possibility for imagining other possibilities that may challenge powerful inequalities.

These writings are also in striking contrast to other forms of anthropological science fiction, particularly those of Ursula K. Le Guin.[12] Although Le Guin indisputably wears the mantle of "anthropological science fiction," particularly for her work from the 1960s and 1970s, there are relatively few similarities between her work and Oliver's. There is little evidence that either ever read (or indeed met) the other; Oliver, for his part, never refers to Le Guin at all, and the closest they ever seem to have gotten was their mutual inclusion in Harlan Ellison's *Again, Dangerous Visions* in 1972. Of course, given Le Guin's emergent feminism and Oliver's unfortunate, Golden Age treatment of women in much of his writing (a tendency he later regretted), it is not particularly surprising that the two of them never seem to have crossed paths. In any case, they represent two very different approaches to anthropology. Although Le Guin utilizes anthropology in her fictions, for example, Craig and Diana Barrow's (1991) analysis of elements of her father's ethnographic notes on Northwest Coast Native Americans in the *Earthsea* cycle, "anthropology" is one of several tools in a portmanteau of resources underlying her astonishing cosmogonies that includes folklore, Jungian psychology, medieval literature and poetry, Taoism, feminism, and ecology. Sometimes, critics like Frederic Jameson and David Ketterer have singled out this eclecticism as a serious flaw in her world-building, as several have done with the Hainish cycle and with *Left Hand of Darkness* in particular. But whatever these critiques, it seems clear that genuine world-building (or what Jameson intriguingly terms "world reduction") has been one of Le Guin's paramount goals. It is therefore entirely consistent that much of her post-Hainish work has taken what Sabia has identified as a more utopian (though still critical) form, the formulation of strikingly different worlds, the *novum* of which rests on their strategic antithesis to worlds that we know (or think we know). The cultural critique in Le Guin's fiction originates precisely in this utopian sense of difference; it is significant that the debate (summarized in Donna R. White's *Dancing with Dragons*) over the default heterosexuality and the gendered pronouns of the Gethenians in *Left Hand of Darkness* revolved around the consistency of their "ambisexuality" as a *novum;* Gethenian sexuality is, in the end, all too familar. Oliver, on the other hand, eschews world-building per se: his later works develop a kind of reverse-acculturation whereby cultural differences are forced upon a moribund West. In this sense, the difference between Oliver and Le Guin can be cast as one of anthropological theory itself; Oliver's works elaborate on theories of acculturation and culture change, while Le Guin seems much closer to the Malinowskian trope of imagining "yourself suddenly set down" on an island of cultural difference ("Argonauts of the Western Pacific"). However, looking over the scope of science fiction, Oliver's "anthropological science fiction"—a fiction of brief encounters illustrating the science of anthropology—seems to have lost out to the grandiose, philosophical world-making of Le Guin. After all, when we think of "anthropological science fiction," it is Le Guin's work—along with that of writers like Frank Herbert, Orson Scott Card, and, more recently, Kim Stanley Robinson—that comes to mind. Oliver's own influence on what has become a subgenre of anthropological science fiction seems slight at best.

Ironically, Oliver's post-1970s work seems closest to many writers to whom the appellation "anthropological science fiction" has never been attached; perhaps this suggests the extent to which anthropology has outpaced the "anthropological" in "anthropological science fiction." Or, perhaps, this has more to do with geography: Oliver's lifelong friendship with Walter Miller, Jr., sprang from the fact that they were two SF writers living in Texas (until Miller moved to Florida). And, throughout the 1980s, Oliver was a regular member of Austin's "Turkey Group," a literary salon that counted Leigh Kennedy, Lewis Shiner, Bruce Sterling, and Lisa Tuttle among its members. Perhaps Oliver did have more in common with these emergent writers than with people like Poul Anderson, whose work he greatly admired but never tried to emulate.[13]

But, in other ways, Oliver's legacy seems strongest in people with only the most tenuous relationship to his work. That the future would be characterized by heterogeneity parallels the works of Octavia Butler and China Miéville, writers who have been variously classified as cyberpunk (Butler) or steampunk (Miéville). Both of them seem to share with Oliver his anticipatory anthropologies. It is not by accident that Octavia Butler was a guest panelist at the 2002 meeting of the American Anthropological Association (Waterston and Vesperi 2003: 12). Well read in anthropology, Butler's work—particularly in the Xenogenesis series—interrogates the constitution of self and other through exploring the boundaries of human and non-human; it is significant that difference is not perceived through the eyes of an objective observer, but instead, as Butler divulged in a 1997 interview with Rowell, experienced as a dramatic (and terrifying) transformation of self. This self-reflexive knowledge of the Other is also very much part of *Kindred* (1979), where Dana arrives at an understanding of US slavery through her own (quite painful) transformation into a slave.

China Miéville—a social scientist with a degree in anthropology—also explores the boundaries between different cultures and human and non-human, although with more of a post-structuralist *jouissance*. Books like *Perdido Street Station* (2001a) revel in a frisson of difference; theorizing from a radical cosmopolitanism, he ultimately seeks the dissolution of stable identity. As Miéville (2001b) writes regarding his fiction,

> But of course cultures aren't monolithic even within themselves. There are a whole mass of conflicting objective interests and impulses embedded in each one. Conflict is not usually the result of some Dread Dark Lord who is threatening things from the outside. Usually there are quite enough tensions cooking up internally to keep things interesting. ... It's paradoxical, trying to depict a world that's simultaneously convincing and utterly fantastic. But one idea united the two impulses: the recognition that things are neat and tidy or monolithic, but complex and contradictory.

Miéville uses this sophisticated understanding of culture and difference to radically subvert hypostatized gender and racial identities and his work, while certainly fantastic, nevertheless critiques a contemporary world of obdurate identities and creeping orientalism.

All of this is not—in an act of peevish disciplinarity—in the way of somehow transferring the label "anthropological science fiction" from Le Guin to Butler and Miéville. Rather, I would suggest that the term be expanded to encompass recent developments in anthropology as well as science fiction. If Oliver can teach us anything, it is that anthropology and science fiction have become steadily more diverse and eclectic in the decades since he began writing in the 1950s. However, as the two disciplines have brachiated into countless experimental schools, movements, and subgenres, new connections between the two have opened up.

CONCLUSIONS

The end of Oliver's life finds him finishing his third western (*The Cannibal Owl*) and plotting a science fiction novel that he hinted in an interview with Tom Knowles would be radically different from all of his previous work.[14] In a way, the Western novel is, in Oliver's hands, and elegant rejoinder to SF. Less concerned with the elaboration of grand theories of human progress à la John W. Campbell, Oliver's three westerns—*The Wolf is My Brother* (1967), *Broken Eagle* (1989), and *The Cannibal Owl* (1994)—dwell on the lives of people caught in the force of culture change that they cannot control. In replaying these nineteenth century, imperial encounters between Comanches, Sioux, Cheyenne, and US soldiers from the perspectives of both Native Americans and Europeans, Oliver in a way opens up the possibility that these tragedies could have been different and suggests that there could have been articulated—along the borders of that frontier—alternatives to genocide.

Over the course of his career, Oliver's work pitted anthropology against SF in myriad, fascinating ways. He would never, however, have replaced one with the other. In fact, he was disdainful of the structural anthropology associated with Levi-Strauss in the 1960s, complaining in the Tom Knowles interview that it was turning anthropologists into literary critics. He would never have conflated his fictions with his ethnographic work; in that respect, he remained faithful to the anthropology of his mentor, Walter Goldschmidt. Nevertheless, Oliver was using science fiction to imagine alternative configurations of power and culture in ways that anticipated a critical anthropology. In turn, Oliver's anthropological, and, importantly, his later experiences with fieldwork in Africa, profoundly informed his SF. It would not be too much to suggest that his experiences with Kamba and the vicissitudes of their lives in a colonized land precipitated a complete rethinking of his science fiction, which in turn influenced the course of his anthropology, for example in his 1981 introductory textbook, *The Discovery of Humanity*. The lesson of Chad Oliver for anthropology is not that we should replace it with science fiction, but that there's something useful in the critical tension between describing cultural difference, on the one hand, and extrapolating cultural possibility, on the other.

Moreover, I would argue that, just as in the way 1950s science fiction and anthropology shared some common assumptions about the power of technology, rational thinking, and the ultimate *telos* of humanity, so, too, over the last fifteen years, certain areas of science fiction and anthropology again suggest productive interrelationships. Science and technology studies, cyborg anthropology, anthropologies of New Reproductive Technologies (NRTs), and the Human Genome Project all examine territories that, while they may bear the imprimatur of science, still are embedded in imagined, discursive spaces of identity, freedom, and power; it is anthropologists and SF writers who will explore these fantastic topographies.

NOTES

This chapter has been previously published as "'Scientifically Valid and Artistically True': Chad Oliver, Anthropology and Anthropological Science Fiction," *Science Fiction Studies* 31(2) (2004): 243–63. The author would like to thank the publication for permission to use the material here.

1. Chad Oliver writes in a 1984 reprint to his novel, *Shadows in the Sun*, "With all respect to Mr. Spock, it might be worth mentioning that we still have no anthropologist aboard the *Enterprise*. I would agree that anthropologists are not the sole curators of wisdom in the human race, but perhaps we could find room for one or two of them when the aliens really hit the fan" (1984: 208). I'd like to think that any anthropologist on the Enterprise would be patterned after Oliver.

2. This and subsequent citations refer to unpublished manuscripts in the Chad Oliver Collection at Cushing Library, Texas A&M University.

3. I have sketched some of these contexts in Collins (2003).

4. In an interview with Hal Hall, Oliver called this "education by irritation" (1989: 75).

5. As one of the *Science Fiction Studies* editors has pointed out, "social engineering" was central to several of Campbell's writers, notably Isaac Asimov. Oliver's contribution was a "cultural engineering" inflected with anthropological theory, although he later derides his efforts as naive. In his notes on his short story "Field Expedient," surrounding the publication of his second anthology of short stories, *The Edge of Forever* (1971), he writes, "Good idea, a bit purple. I was so confident about successfully manipulating cultures" (COC: Box 1[50]).

5. Thanks to an anonymous reviewer for pointing to the Merdosi's ESP as a distinctly Campbell-ian conceit. Oliver certainly continues his "dialogue" with Campbell in this novel, and it is significant that these people in no way represent some successor state to Homo sapiens. Rather, they are just different: cultural relativism applied to science fiction.

6. Cultural ecology, as Michael Herzfeld summarizes, contends that "features of human society and culture can be explained in terms of the environments in which they have developed" (2001: 175).

7. For example, the publication of Malinowski's Trobriand fieldnotes, *A Diary in the Strict Sense of the Term* (1967), revealed a man beset by quotidian loneliness, culture shock, and despair—very different from the heroic ethnographer who appears in *Argonauts of the Western Pacific* (1922).

8. In a 1989 interview with Thomas Knowles, Oliver reflected that this period of field research had caused him to rethink many of his ideas.

9. Both of which he worked on in Kenya.

10. This is something Oliver (COC: Box 9[20]) has remarked on in connection with another story inspired by his Kenya research, "A Stick for Harry Eddington" (1965b):

    When I was in Africa doing research with the Kamba, I was struck by how eager many of these people were to change places with us. I should have known better, but I had expected to find races of the old stereotypes: a "primitive" people grimly clinging to traditional patterns and much given to wistful backward glances at the Good Old Days.... I could see attractive things about the way they lived because I could contrast them with what I had known; they saw only the trappings of power through the eyes of men who had known all their lives what it was like to be powerless.

11. In this anthropological parable, Lee must enter the house of "Gilbert McAllister" in order to discover the world beyond the domed city. J. Gilbert McAllister was, of course, Oliver's undergraduate anthropology teacher and, presumably, the voice who addresses Lee about the people beyond the dome.

12. Michael Bishop is another writer whose work, while certainly anthropological, is nevertheless very different from Oliver's. For example, Bishop's *Transfigurations* (1980) uses ethnography as the backdrop for the psychological transformations of its protagonist, in a way reminiscent of Joseph Conrad. This tendency can also be read in works like *No Enemy But Time* (1982). In this, Bishop's "anthropology" resonates with the self-reflexive work of James Clifford.

13. Oliver's membership in the "Turkey City" group seemed to have stimulated his own work and he genuinely seems to have been flattered by his acceptance by a younger generation of writers. It is uncertain, however, how much influence Shiner, Sterling, and company had on Oliver's fiction. Likewise, Oliver's contributions to the writings of other members remain unacknowledged.

14. It seems unlikely that we will ever know what work he was thinking about. He was working on a semi-autobiographical novel about growing up in Texas ("The Sounds of the Earth"), but this was demonstrably *not* science fiction.

Chapter 4

Close Encounters of the Anthropological Kind

Reflecting on his life in France, so very different than his Genevan youth, Jean-Jacques Rousseau likened it to "some strange planet" (quoted in Kurasawa 2004: 1). Like many Enlightenment thinkers, Rousseau relied on cultural alterity (in his case, his deployment of the "savage") in order to stimulate what Fuyuki Kurasawa (2004) has called the "ethnological imagination." Different lifeworlds juxtaposed to the European present could be used to critique (Rousseau, Herder) or legitimate (Smith, Locke, Hobbes) the new, bourgeois order. But Rousseau's invocation of life on an alien world seems to stretch the hyperbole too far. Isn't the "alien" by definition beyond the asymptote of cultural alterity? After all: "Homo sum: humani nihil a me alienum puto."

And yet, for the very reason that it represents some absolute alterity, many have found the figure of the alien useful. It offered Kant, for example, an ideal tablet on which to figure the emerging, bourgeois *mensch*. In *Anthropology from a Pragmatic Point of View,* Kant introduces variously uncanny aliens possessed by strange powers (for example,what we would now refer to as telepathy) in order to delineate the moral life of the civilized. But this is only conjecture and metaphor; as David Clark (2001: 201) points out, Kant's *Anthropology* falters in its description of "man" for lack of a "nonterrestrial rational being." There is no truly exterior perspective on Homo sapiens. Kant, of course, presses on, but the project can only remain incomplete; the alien, Clark (210–211) reminds us, still haunts the *Anthropology:* "To put it differently, the fiction of 'man' finds an uncanny simulacrum in the science fiction of the aliens whose very absence keeps 'man' from being known as an experienced 'fact.' 'Man' is not only indebted to the simulated alien; 'he' is a simulation of himself, a trope for the conflation between what the *Anthropology* promises via the circuit of the alien and what it must posit as already in place to make that promise." So, lacking the alien Other, the anthropological project must remain open-ended and unfinished, both in terms of "man" as a continuously unfolding project and in terms of the alien, who may yet offer us the ultimate perspective on ourselves.

Like Kant, anthropologists, for the most part, have continued the task of describing Homo sapiens without the alien animus. Mead, although certainly a science fiction reader, did not pin her hopes for the future on the arrival of beneficent aliens. Her prognostications were grounded in the experience of people on Earth; however much the idea of lunar colonization might have excited her, it was an enterprise that humans would undertake alone, although Mead, like the *Mars* novels of Kim Stanley Robinson, saw the potential for a generation gap that, as I will suggest below, belongs to a strain of anthropological thought *producing* the alien (Williams 1995: 379). Chad Oliver's writings, on the other hand, frequently used the alien as a foil for the critique of human cultures.

In these works, though, the alien hovers beyond the asymptote of anthropological vision, conjured up for rhetorical effect but ultimately subordinated to the more sacerdotal interests of anthropology as a serious, scientific pursuit. But what if the alien had been there all along? Like the monolith excavated under lunar regolith in Stanley Kubrick's *2001,* the alien may have been exerting its alien-ness on our future figurations of culture for some time.

This chapter delves into an alien, that, at times, creeps into the center of anthropological inquiry, the disquieting entrée of the ultimate Other. Alfred Russel Wallace, as Peter Pels (2003: 255) has shown, attributed human evolution to the beneficent influence of spirits, including "intelligences other than God." Others, like anthropologists involved in "Project Grendel," sought the terrestrial alien in their search for extant, non-human hominids like "Sasquatch," while the last proponent of 19th-century, racist anthropology, Carleton S. Coon, is said to have lectured on "yeti" (Roth 2005: 65). In a more quotidian vein, Gregory Bateson extended his studies of cognition to incorporate dolphins (Bateson 1979). For the rest of anthropology, aliens have led a more sepulchral existence, winding their way though anthropological fictions and elaborate *gedanken,* supplementing more serious work with occasional, speculative flights.

But we might see these reveries more seriously as well. In another way, the incommensurable and uncanny alien, like Michel Serres's "demon," enables the study of humanity through its active exclusion—the *elenchos* of the alien. And just as the Other, for Emmanuel Lévinas, is a figure of desire (and of horror), so the alien, lying beyond vision and sense, acts as a promise (or a threat) of what we might become. The following chapter, then, takes Kant's *Anthropology* as an entry into what might be called the moieties of the alien: (1) the alien as the ultimate, asymptotic "Other" of humanity, and (2) the alien as humanity's future. In the course of this inquiry, I incorporate exactly those ludic sources that have made up, as Richard Handler (2000) has quipped, our "excluded ancestors," with the intent of showing that these, like the Derridean supplement, are ultimately constitutive of the anthropology project, not only that first contact with the alien is already a fait accompli, but that our understanding of what Battaglia is calling "E.T. Culture" is absolutely necessary before we can undertake an investigation of contemporary, Earth culture (Battaglia 2005).

THE ANTHROPOLOGICAL ALIEN

Since at least the growth of SETI (Search for Extraterrestrial Intelligence) research in the work of Giuseppe Cocconi, Philip Morrison, Frank Drake, and others, anthropologists have tried to advise their science counterparts. After all, NASA's earliest efforts at formulating first contact protocols—the 1961 Brookings reports commissioned by NASA and submitted to the eighty-seventh Congress—contextualized first contact in anthropological precedent: "Anthropological files contain many examples of societies, sure of their place in the universe, which have disintegrated when they had to associate with previously unfamiliar societies espousing different ideas and different lifeways; others that survived such an experience usually did so by paying the price of changes in values and attitudes and behaviors." While anthropologists—until recently—have had little input into astrobiology per se, there have been several contributions over the decades from anthropologists consisting of analogous examples of culture contact from the anthropological record.

In the 1970s, for example, a series of symposia sponsored by the American Anthropological Association resulted in an edited collection of papers, *Cultures Beyond the Earth: the Role of Anthropology in Outer Space.* Informed by the legacy of indigenous peoples at the hands of Western colonials, papers on first contact elaborated on the obligations of Earth representatives toward aliens. As Barbara Moskowitz (1975: 65) weighed in: "Our confrontations, on the other hand, will most likely be with life forms as yet unfamiliar to us—physically, biologically, perhaps even psychologically. The realization of past mistakes as well as the facts and interpretations gleaned from previous cross-cultural encounters are necessary to command in ourselves attitudes of respect for the lives and life styles of interplanetary inhabitants." Efforts at contact had to be tempered by both knowledge of past mistakes as well the kind of cultural relativism developed by the anthropologists over the course of the 20th century. As Ashley Montagu (1973: 25) suggested at a NASA symposium held at Boston University in 1972: "I do not think that we should wait until the encounter occurs; we should do all in our power to prepare ourselves for it. The manner in which we first meet may determine the character of all of our subsequent relations. Let us never forget the great impact we have upon innumerable peoples on this Earth—peoples of our own species who trusted us, befriended us and whom we destroyed by our thoughtlessness and insensitivity to their needs and vulnerabilities." Of course, we might ask whether "thoughtlessness and insensitivity" will be the issue, or will first contact, like past encounters, be overdetermined by pedestrian greed, desire, and hatred?

One way anthropologists have developed to inculcate these attitudes has been through role-play. CONTACT, an annual conference founded in 1983 by anthropologist Jim Funaro, brings together scientists, anthropologists, and writers in order to speculate on extraterrestrial life and, in a series of role-playing scenarios derived from Role Playing Games like *Dungeons and Dragons*, enact first contact. This eventually developed into two, separate events, "Cultures of the Imagination" (COTI), an event open to all comers, and the by-invitation-only Bateson Project. Funaro (1994) reflects on the first Bateson Project session at CONTACT in 1983:

> The aliens were sea creatures, a new taxon combining many characteristics we find in the cetaceans, crustaceans and mollusks of Earth.... We named the species the Alchemists, because their bodies were chemical factories, producing complex nucleotide messages as well as wide spectrum sound. They filled the seas of their world with song and pheromones.
>
> The humans were refugees from a destroyed Earth. The colony had been traveling in space in search of a new home for many generations, during which time they had not only developed a unique, self-contained culture but had also evolved biologically.

This particular simulation, with the humans first encountering aliens in their water-filled spacecraft, ends in a desultory way. But the point of the simulation is not, of course, to predict alien morphology or ethology, but to evoke and interrogate the human response. As the anthropologist Dirk van der Elst later recounted in an article in *Omni* (Ferrell 1992), "COTI players reflect their own cultures, no matter what they think they're doing. But what you can do with COTI is create a substitute human species, a species that can do all the things humans could do if they hadn't been such bastards." Van der Elst, along with others like Paul Bohannan, has incorporated COTI-style role-playing into his classroom for precisely this reason: it offers not only a way to apply anthropological ideas to a novel situation, but additionally excavates the assumptions that have informed encounters with non-Western others (Bohannan 1992).[1]

But the more vital role for anthropologists appears to be gadfly to SETI projects.[2] Many others have, of course, been skeptical of SETI research, including scientists like Enrico Fermi and Ernst Mayr, who doubt the chances of either detecting a signal or establishing contact, and most importantly, members of the US Congress who cancelled NASA's High Resolution Microwave Survey in 1993 (Garber 1999). Others have pointed out that a truly alien intelligence will most likely be incommensurable from our human perspective (Cooper 2004; Werth 1998). On the other hand, the role of anthropologists has been less to cast aspersions at the science of SETI than interrogate the way SETI scientists have constructed their would-be alien interlocutors, from the striking, neo-Spencerianism of the Drake Equation, where "advanced technology" and "civilization" are very nearly synonymous, to theories like John Ball's "Zoo hypothesis," which holds that aliens are silently watching us, and the "Deadly Probes Hypothesis," which suggests that some galactic power might be systematically destroying advanced civilizations—a paranoid's explanation for the Fermi paradox (that is, "where are they?") (McConnell 2001). All of these say a great deal more about the United States and its Machiavellian machinations than they say about aliens: shades of the Cold War and the Patriot Act, to be sure.

Anthropologists like Michael Ashkenazi (1995: 514), echoing, really, Boasians writing almost a century before, have questioned the technological and economic assumptions underlying SETI research. Perhaps ETI (Extraterrestrial Intelligence) doesn't have a "natural" proclivity for space travel and for scanning radio waves at the natural, spectral emission of hydrogen. "An alternative view may be termed a *culturalist* one, which views the entire institution of space exploration as a cultural choice, one alternative among others. This view essentially assumes that there are a number of alternative cultural institutions that can be developed." This is hardly fatal to SETI, of course. These critiques merely underline the necessity to adjust the Drake Equation by both expanding what we mean by "civilization" and by decoupling that definition from the techno-scientific trajectory of Western capitalism. Indeed, many of the same anthropologists who have been critical of cultural assumptions built into SETI research have signed onto the "Invitation to ETI" (ieti.org), a website inviting aliens already on Earth to make contact with the undersigned scientists and intellectuals.

> As we think about extraterrestrial intelligence or alien intelligence, we realize that your presence here could take various forms. For instance, we realize that

you could be present here in the form of an extraordinarily advanced interstellar probe or alien robot or superintelligence. Or you could be a biological flesh-and-blood being. Or some combination of the two. Perhaps you have evolved even further. You might be an energy field, a point of consciousness, or something else far beyond our current scientific understanding. Whatever form you take, we welcome you and we seek dialogue.[3]

More than, perhaps, the scientific understanding of aliens, the anthropologists signing on to "Invitation to ETI" are wary of the *cultural* understandings of aliens that presuppose anthropomorphic aliens possessed of the same drives and faculties as the scientists who hope to contact them. Reed Riner (2000: 129), for example, urges scientists to look beyond "West and rest" encounters in order to evoke other possibilities with outcomes other than "the emasculating subordination of one party by the other or the destruction of one or mutually by both parties." There have been many, mutually beneficial contacts between different groups of humans; these—rather than the various Western colonizations and genocides of the last five hundred years—should be our model for alien contact.

It is to this point that anthropologists have returned most often: the cultural contexts imbricating apperceptions of the alien. Robert Bartholomew, for example, analyzes UFO sightings as an example of the social construction of reality. Pointing out that nineteenth-century UFO sightings (the "airship craze" of 1897–1899) had nothing to do with aliens, Bartholomew (1991: 7–8) suggests that the association of UFOs with aliens in the 1950s coincides with a rejection of over-rationalization at a time of particular stress from the threat of nuclear Armageddon. In this context, aliens become nonce gods in an effort to evoke alternative realities, in Bartholomew's words, "the secularized Western collective unconscious and its attempt to plausibly resurrect the power of these earlier gods." UFO sightings are, in other words, twentieth-century mythologies reflecting the Gestalt of a paranoid—but still hopeful—age. On the other hand Susan Lepselter (2005: 273) suggests we look to alien abduction stories against a backdrop of economic insecurity, libertarian ideology, and Harry Braverman's "deskilling" thesis: "In the rural American West, fierce ideologies of independence and self-reliance collide with other, unspoken narratives—the inarticulate disappointments of experience, the specter of your own other life that never took shape in the way, somehow, it should have. The ordinary and fantastic stories can converge in the vague sense of some impenetrable source of abduction, some agent of theft, some plot by the powers that be." Lepselter evokes what might be called a poetics of alien abduction, even arranging her informant's interviews into a kind of blank verse. This treatment underscores two themes anthropologists have stressed in their scholarship on alien abduction, namely: (1) that

UFO abduction stories are not explained by reference to DSM categories (for example, schizophrenia), and that (2) whatever the validity of the stories themselves, they additionally articulate cultural frisson at the turn of the twenty-first century. Indeed, Deborah Battaglia's *E.T. Culture* (2005) generalizes the alien into our common discourse; we live in the aftermath of (cultural) first contact.

Anthropologists, in the spirit of cultural relativism, have suspended disbelief on the existence of aliens or the validity of abduction stories, but this leads us ineluctably, back to the Earth itself, to ask questions not about the alien, but about the peoples and discourses of the alien. Whether or not aliens have contacted the Earth, it's the human response that concerns anthropologists most. This was certainly the case at a 1999 astrobiology conference, where anthropologists met together with other scientists to consider human responses to extraterrestrial life. Their resolutions (NASA 1999: 9) were inflected with anthropological insights:

> How can we formulate a cohesive plan of action for short-term and long-term responses to Extraterrestrial Intelligence (ETI)? Possible strategies include the following. (1) Developing scenario-contingent strategies for managing discovery and its aftermath; undertaking studies based on analogues in the humanities and history. (2) The social and behavioral sciences, and science fiction to determine likely reactions. (3) Undertaking carefully planned cross-cultural polls and other empirical studies. (4) Exploring the capacity of religion as a resource to absorb impact of discovery and maintain beneficial relations with ETI.

But, given the premise that "Aliens have already been assimilated into every life" (Dean 1997), do we need to wait for first contact? We have already been inexorably changed through our interactions with the alien imaginary. In other words, there's no need to wait; we (and that "we" is always already suspect) have already responded to the aliens, never mind that they may never have been there to begin with.

WE HAVE MET THE ALIEN AND SHE IS US

Like Chad Oliver, Morton Klass juggled at least two identities—one as an anthropologist of religion at Columbia University, the other as a science fiction writer, brother to Phillip Klass (aka William Tenn). And yet—again like Oliver—Klass used science fiction to extrapolate on and to interrogate anthropological theory. For example, the protagonist of Klass's "Earthman's Burden" (1989: 217) is Arthur Morales, an anthropologist accompanying a team to contact a galactic empire. When the team decides to endorse an

Earth takeover of the alien empire, Morales balks and is promptly killed as a traitor to humanity. Luckily, he is quickly revived by his alien hosts, who fill him in on the scam; they want the Earth to take everything over: "The Trogish viceroy wiggled his ears contentedly. 'That's right. The galaxy is a smoothly running affair, you see. All it needs is a few individuals on each planet to keep things moving. Isn't it fair that the youngest, most backward species be given the job? After all, someone has to do it, and the older races obviously can do much more important things. Besides, it helps the new-comers to mature.'" Besides skewering the Western equation of technology with progress (and, in another way, legitimating it), Klass neatly captures another leitmotif in the anthropology of the alien: the possibility that we might become the alien in the course of our "own" evolution and develop-ment, what Krafft Ehricke calls the "extraterrestrial imperative" to migrate into space (Finney 1992: 113).

This evolutionary teleology is embedded in twentieth-century plans for space travel and space colonization. Initially, this was defined according to the post-War military-industrial complex; Wernher Von Braun's *Das Marspro-jekt* (1952), a work of fiction completed in the US but first published in Ger-many, envisioned a military flotilla colonizing Mars in the name of the West, an extension of Fredrick Jackson Turner's "frontier thesis" more recently shared by Robert Zubrin, who rhapsodizes over the expansionist urge in *The Case for Mars* (Klerkx 2004). However, the evisceration of the Apollo program in the 1970s opened the way for what D.W. Kilgore has called a "second-wave astrofuturism" composed of scientists and laity unconnected with the defense industry.

Some of these, like the "first-wave" astrofuturists before them, saw the colonization of space as the best way to preserve putatively "American" val-ues, such as Gerard O'Neill's L-5 colonies—so-called because of their loca-tion at the fifth Lagrangian point. As Kilgore (2003: 159) explains, "Like many Americans of his generation, O'Neill believed that the American way of life could only be guaranteed by plenty of elbow room. His response to the pessimistic limits-to-growth debate advocated the colonization of a terri-tory that would allow national growth to continue ad infinitum, guarantee-ing an eternal regeneration of the social, political, and economic constraints of American values." For O'Neill, that even included colonies segregated by race and religion, dismal echoes of the segregated suburbs developed after World War II. According to this logic, the "Dyson sphere," the establish-ment of millions of colonies creating an artificial biosphere around the sun, represents the ultimate sprawl.

But not everyone saw space colonization as the imperious continuation of the US present; anthropologists saw it as an opportunity to produce cultural alterity and to experiment with different, cultural configurations. Mead saw the Apollo program as productive of new perspectives on the Earth, "the development of a new context within which we can look for viable solutions," and theorized about the "generation gap" moon colonization would precipitate (Collins 2005b; Mead 2005: 250). And in the 1970s, Magoroh Maruyama and Arthur Harkins (1975: 13) created a cottage industry around theorizing cultural engineering for space colonization: "In the era of extraterrestrial communities, we will have hitherto unknown cultural options. In such communities, many of the constraints which restrict life on Earth are removed. Temperature, seasons, weather, artificial gravity, etc, can be set at will, and new types of cultures become possible. We will be in a position to first invent new cultural patterns and then choose material conditions and community design to fit this desire cultural pattern." To Maruyama, Harkins, and other "cultural futurists," space colonization was best undertaken by small groups patterned after "tribes" or "bands," maximizing adaptive advantage through generating what are in essence in situ cultural experiments (Funaro 1994). Ben Finney and Eric Jones (1985: 99) imagine "tribal groups of at least 500 citizens" inhabiting the interior of comets; as they slowly diffuse into the galaxy, each would develop autochthonous cultural mores and rituals. These have been accompanied by somewhat less romantic studies of small group interaction in isolated research stations in Antarctica and near the Arctic Circle, undertaken with the intent of providing data on social and cultural challenges in long-term space travel (Johnson and Finney 1986; Palinkas 1990).

But, Finney and Jones caution, there are also attendant dangers; could we become aliens ourselves? Initially human settlements could, over the course of thousands of years, brachiate into entirely different species:

> There are innumerable environments out there providing countless niches to exploit, first by humans and then by the multitudinous descendant species. By expanding through space we will be embarking on an adventure that will spread an explosive speciation of intelligent life as far as technology or limits placed by any competing life forms originating elsewhere will allow. Could the radiation of evolving, intelligent life through space be the galactic destiny of this Earth creature we have called the exploring animal? (101)

That is, is there a tension between fulfilling "our" galactic destiny while simultaneously becoming alien to "us"? If we see "cosmicisation" as the destiny of "humanity" (or at least portions of it), then there seems to be a limit to that expansion. We might, in other words, utilize the alien to know ourselves, or to realize our own Spencerian teleologies, but to actually become the alien is to leave the human behind. This is certainly a theme in UFO abduction stories, where women are impregnated and the hybrid human-alien fetuses are harvested from their bodies, expressing, as Jodi Dean (1997) and others have pointed out, "anxiety about breeding, miscegenation, and hybridity, about the collapse of distinctions between the alien and ourselves."

But not everyone sees this hybridity with dread. There are, as many anthropologists have pointed out, emancipatory possibilities in our conjoining with the alien. For example, Stefan Helmreich (2001: 341) has been studying the anthropological possibilities suggested by scientific discourses around Archaea, hyperthermophilic microorganisms that are anomalous in many ways, not the least of which is their disregard for traditional taxonomies of phylum. "The scrambling of the biogenetic phylogenetic signal that these creatures enact has implications for the integrity of Darwin's link between genealogy and taxonomy—as well, perhaps, for the biogenetic imaginary outlined by Schneider." Archaea, as "agents of lateral gene transfer, installing alienness at many sites around the root of life," undermine not only Linnean certainties, but also confound the species-being. If we are also the sum of our alien parts (for example, mitochondria), then what is the human? It is by now a familiar Deleuzean maneuver to champion assemblage and involution over filiation and descent. And for Gilles Deleuze and Félix Guattari (1987), these hold the promise of challenging stable (and exclusive) ontologies of all sorts with "assemblages that are neither those of the family nor of religion nor of the State." Yet, there are limits to this as well; conjoining with aliens might grant us heretofore unknown perspectives, but becoming the alien is decidedly recidivistic, simply reinscribing the hypostasis of the Self onto the body of the Other. Jane Bennett (2001: 31) prefers to refer to these hybrid states as "crossings" in order to avoid "the image of static entities coming together to form a compound." That is, it does us little good to "become" the alien without recombining with the human.

Oliver (1983: 27), in one of his last stories, makes this point. A party from Earth encounters an O'Neill (a torus-shaped space colony) that has, presumably, been isolated for generations. Inside, a single, remaining colonist—no longer quite human—awaits the landing. Combining his mind (Caroth) with that of the landing party's archaeologist (Rick), Caroth/Rick makes his plans:

> He had an enormous advantage now. He could see into their minds. There was much he could do.
>
> He could stall the destruction of the O'Neill indefinitely.
>
> He could work with the remnant of his people.
>
> He could bring something back to Earth more precious than artifacts. He had lived in the past, he had professional training. He was a link with all the vanished generations. He *knew* them. Not just on the O'Neill. On Earth.

That is, the human, having become alien, must recombine with the human in order to manifest her alien power. In one way, this is entirely consistent with Deleuzean involution. As Bennett (2001: 31) writes, "Every new assemblage reverberates back upon old atoms and changes them." Every "becoming animal," in the sense of Henri Bergson, changes our perspectives on what came before, seeding the Earth with alien and thereby creating an almost-Kantian (with emphasis on the almost) perspective back on the human, "almost" because the desirability of the alien perspective is inflected with twentieth-century knowledge that these stable ontologies hide the stealth crossing that enable this impossible perspective in the first place.

Extrapolating on the non-terrestrial only to fold this back to the terrestrial is an august tradition of cultural critique in anthropology which, so it goes, "makes the familiar strange, the exotic quotidian" (Clifford and Marcus 1986: 2), alter-ego to twentieth-century surrealism (Clifford 1981). But, reduced to this brute algebra, making one into the other may titillate, but cannot ultimately transform; the "familiar" and "strange" continue to revolve ceaselessly, one about the other. Micaela di Leonardo (1998: 61) has critiqued what she calls the "anthropological gambit," that is, "cross-cultural vignettes which reify the pool hall vision of cultural difference, place Others at a temporal distance, and thus efface the questions of history and power on both poles of the contrast." That is, "familiar" and "strange" are each eclipsed in the umbra of the other, the messiness of their relation relegated to a stable binary. What the anthropology of the alien suggests is the necessity of more complex transformation, where, perhaps, the "strange" and the "familiar" interpenetrate each other, where the "crossings" between them are ultimately stochastic.

In addition, we might utilize this realization to critique the ways "the Other" has occupied the "alien" slot, a familiar, racist trope in science fiction that has, over the decades, traded in "traditional Orientalism" for a "techno-orientalism" that erects the scaffolding of alien futures on the racialized bodies of Asian characters (Sohn 2017). Afrofuturist artists like Sun Ra have utilized identification with "the alien" in order to undermine this "othering" to break through the binarism of the US race-caste system (Tsitsos 2014). And this movement toward alien transformation and the posthuman has its emancipatory side, as Octavia Butler has explored in her "Xenogensis" trilogy (although here, too, is domination from an alien power) (Bogue 2011).

Perhaps better than the endlessly invoked "strange and familiar" trope, might be something along the lines of Freud's "The Uncanny" (1919), where the "homely" (*heimlich*) transforms into its uncanny (*unheimlich*), in the process unsettling both. First, the familiar (animate objects, a house, a city) prove strange and uncanny. Second, the uncanny proves familiar after all. Third, the familiar and the uncanny triangulate uneasily, creating the dream-like state which confuses the ordinary with the extraordinary, the animate with the inanimate, the mythological with the quotidian. Having discovered the alien, and then the alien-human, anthropologists by degrees diagnose the human-alien, that is, the humans that were never as familiar as "we" thought. Might it not be the case that human was rather alien all along?

This is really what we should read into anthropological work with NASA and SETI: not that the cultural Other is like an alien (a source of legitimation for the current round of xenophobia in the Western imaginary), but that the self can *be alien* (cautioning us against easy generalizations) and also *become alien* (the promise of a future productive of alterity rather than stale homogeneity). It is this promise that fuels the last chapters in this book.

NOTES

1. Thanks to an anonymous reviewer for pointing out the changes in CONTACT over the years. No longer held at NASA Ames, the future of CONTACT is in doubt: this year's (2007) CONTACT has been cancelled. COTI has developed into a high school educational project and the Bateson Project, to my knowledge, has not been held for some time.

2. There have been sessions devoted to SETI at both the 2005 and 2006 American Anthropological Association Annual Conferences that have handily demonstrated contributions of anthropologists while at the same time showcasing the anthropologically interesting questions SETI research raises.

3. Again, thanks to an anonymous reviewer for pointing out that "Invitation to ETI" presumes an alien intelligence with internet access and a proclivity for search engines.

Chapter 5

Playing Games with Futurology

Joshua: Shall we play a game?
David: Oh!
Jennifer: I think it missed him.
David: Yeah. Weird isn't it? Love to. How about Global Thermonuclear War?
Joshua: Wouldn't you prefer a nice game of chess?
David: Later. Right now let's play Global Thermonuclear War.
Joshua: Fine.
(*Wargames* 1983)

My overwhelming impression of futurology comes from the work of Herman Kahn; his 1960 book *On Thermonuclear War* horrified a generation with its frank discussion of nuclear war survival strategies, and it simultaneously introduced the world to the kind of scenario-driven futures research that Kahn had developed in his capacity as resident genius at the RAND corporation. This is said to have inspired Stanley Kubrick's *Dr. Strangelove,* in turn inspiring representations of supercomputers, like the fictional WOPR (War Operation Plan Response, above) controlling the US nuclear arsenal at NORAD (North American Air Defense). Both human and computer are coldly calculating as they scroll through simulations for the end of the world, quantitatively playing out the endgame, comparing lists of causalities, assessing damage to infrastructure, et cetera, using war games, game theory, the prisoner's dilemma, and so on, to domesticate the unthinkable. This was the "game" of the future: playing "what if ..." with the many real and imagined enemies of US foreign policy. To be sure, with its military connections, RAND continues to produce properly Strange-lovian titles, for example, *Striking First: Preemptive and Preventative Attack in U.S. National Security Policy* (Mueller et al 2006), that are more sophisticated extrapolations on US policy.

But the doomsday scenarios Kahn was most famous for, or that his colleagues at RAND subsequently developed (Theodore Gordon, Olaf Helmer, et cetera), are said to have fallen out of favor: the kinds of "futures" thinking that animate Kahn's *The Year 2000* or *The Next Two Hundred Years*. Indeed, as David Rejeski and Robert Olson (2006) point out, much of the futures work within government—the Futures Research Group of the Congressional Research Service or the Office of Technology Assessment (OTA)—has been eliminated. The reasons for this were discussed earlier in this book: there's no need to prognosticate about the future when it's not going to be any different than it is now. All we need is the actuarial table in the age of globalization. "The future" as an idea has been replaced with a linear model that replaces the future as "difference" with the future as "increasing magnitude." This is the dull algebra (that nevertheless excited people in the 1990s) of Moore's Law—transistor capacity doubles every ten years, or, in its more recent formulation, chip density doubles every eighteen months, but there is little stochastic to enliven these formulations.

Much of what is considered "cutting edge" in global capitalism, moreover, has little patience with Kondratieff waves or the future conceived as the long duree. Futures markets, hedge funds, and derivatives instruments of all kinds derive value from extremely attenuated "futures" with an ultimate horizon measured in seconds rather than centuries (LiPuma and Lee 2004). "Derivatives" markets proliferate in the interstices of Newtonian time, and, like the light nanoseconds in which spacetime dilations are measured, exist only in the flickering communication gap between governments, banks, and markets; thus, the deft (and computer-driven) exploitation of pricing differences in different markets can be used to squeeze profit out of a future where, eventually, things will return to equilibrium. This kind of "speed-up" future is hardly amenable to the sorts of leisured temporalizations produced in the comfort of think tanks like RAND or the Institute for Global Futures.

To be sure, we can find little anthropological in these Realpolitik futures anyway. Indeed, in this context, it is possible to say that "the future" and anthropology "have been like two ships passing in the night" (Razak and Cole 1995: 277). Although this book is evidence of the long-standing involvement of anthropology in the future, "futurology" as a formal discipline has long been the province of other social sciences. Which, of course, tells us a great deal about the kinds of "future" that are important. Without playing on the "anthropological gambit" too heavily, I still note that futurists are never called in to discuss the future of shamanism, or of magic; nor are they asked to prognosticate on the future of subsistence agriculture or ayurvedic medicine. The answer, sadly, is that most in futures research consider these—as E. B. Tylor did a century before—as the very antithesis of the future, something that with luck will wither away in the cold light of GMO (Genetically Modified Organisms) agri-business and the World Trade Organization. And it is no mistake that the people who make "anthropological predictions"— for example, the tired, Malthusian refrains in Jared Diamond's *Collapse* (2005)—are themselves poaching on the field of anthropology (Diamond is a geographer).

But at the same time, one might make the argument that anthropology has been a curious supplement to the growth of twentieth-century futurology. Consider *The Next 200 Years* (Kahn et al 1976: 140) with its careful (albeit linear) projections of energy costs, food production, environment pressures, and so on. None of it would make much of an impact were there not also narratives:

> We expect that with the passage of time there will be fewer struggles over life-and-death or critical health decisions and sever economic damage, but instead efforts will be increasingly focused on aesthetic or quality-of-life issues—perhaps even relatively marginal ones. Only fanatics will feel personally defeated (or see a disaster for mankind) each time a power plant is sited, an oil tract leased or a pipeline built.... But probably by 10 to 15 years from now, almost certainly by the year 2000, it is very likely that we will be able to look back with great pride in our accomplishments. We will breathe clean air, drink directly from rivers and enjoy pleasing landscapes.

It is easy to dismiss these just-so stories with the laugh of a cynic; certainly there is a regular industry out there in future-bashing (see Cristol 2003). It is a regular theme in New Year's feature pieces in newspapers to dredge up the failed predictions of pundits past, part of the "future nostalgia" that Harding et al diagnose (Rosenberg and Harding 2005). But what is interesting here is how much predictions of the future-however grounded in quantitative modeling, game theory, et cetera—depend for their power on narratives of what being human will be like in the future. Could Gerard O'Neill's *The High Frontier* (1977) have been as successful if there hadn't have been narratives on future life-ways interspersed between discussions of mass drivers and hydroponics (Kilgore 2003)? Or, in another more recent example, Warren Wagar's *A Short History of the Future* (1999) also hinges on narratives of future depressions, future cosmopolitanisms, future socialisms, à la *News From Nowhere*.

What if these more quantitative theories of the future—from econometric modeling to ecological predictions—depended a priori on their cultural tropes, rather than simply using first-person or epistolary narratives as a means to illustrate their desiccated tables of production units and parts-per-million? And this is where anthropology comes in, as interlocutor and as critic. The following chapter briefly addresses futurology from this perspective, but this is not meant in any way to be a summary of futurology or futurism: people interested in that are urged to attend to excellent histories on the subject (Bell 1997).

QUANTIFYING THE FUTURE

The most well-known sorts of futures are the predictive sort—the 52-year cycles discovered by Nikolai Kondratieff (the Kondratieff long wave) that have been used to predict the boom and bust of the capitalist system over the past century (Westwood 2000). This has been recently extended to the world capitalist system as a whole, notably by the economist Carl Dassbach (1993), and by Immanel Wallertstein (2000), who finds in them a vindication for his own world-system theories. As Wallerstein explains (2000: 250): "The period 1945 to today is that of a typical Kondratieff cycle of the capitalist world-economy, which has had as always two parts: an A-phase or upward swing or economic expansion that went from 1945 to 1976–73, and a B-phase or downward swing or economic contraction that has been going from 1967–73 to today and probably will continue on for several more years." The idea, of course, is hardly a new one, and underlies the unilinear narratives of Oswald Spengler, Arnold Toynbee, Karl Marx, and others, all of whom traced the history of nations or of political economy in sinusoid cycles of boom and bust.

Of course, these are backed up by economic data, but the narrative remains the same: a cybernetic monologue on positive and negative feedback, together with the inevitable "corrections" that have been naturalized as inevitable in neoliberal cosmology. From Wallerstein (2000: 257–258): "The capitalist world economy has long maintained itself, as a system does, by mechanisms that restore equilibrium every time its processes move away from it. The equilibrium is never restored immediately, but only after a sufficient deviation from the norm occurs, and, of course, it is never restored perfectly."

Wallerstein's is a more critical application of first-generation cybernetics, with the system never returning to the absolute equilibrium of the homeostat, yet its debt to cybernetics is clear. And other simulations, generating future predictions mostly from linear projections (and linear regressions) based on the past, are following the same, general method. Thus, the World3 simulation, developed for the Club of Rome, unfolds according to that time-worn, procrustean bed. That is, World3 is essentially a Malthusian growth model: growth precipitates exponential demand, depleting the world's resources and precipitating ecological and economic disaster.

What Kondratieff long waves suggest is a fundamentally conservative approach. After all, it hardly motivates one to revolutionary action if one already knows one is locked within a sinusoid pattern anyway—just ride the

long wave, as it were. On the other had, the neo-Malthusian prognostications of the Club of Rome or Paul Ehrlich's *The Population Bomb* could well
be utilized for progressive causes (and have been), in this case, activism and
policy designed to address imminent catastrophe. Of course, these are all
structured in the familiar tale of the fecund underclass, with its spiraling
birth rates, the barely concealed racism of which continues to dog international population control groups today.

However, as Reed Riner (1991: 299) summarizes, whether reactionary
or progressive, these simulations share a dogged linearity: "At any moment
in its progress the model may be arrested to display—once the numbers
are decrypted—an image of the future. The kinds of images are, as econo-
mist-futurist Robert Theobald has often remarked in private communica-
tions, 'surprise-free, zero imagination' images of the future." In a world of
frequent surprises, simulations ensure that the future we envision will be a
bland recapitulation of the past. But to say that they are obsolete is to ignore
the continued usefulness of World3 and other global simulations (remember
that global warming?) (cf. Meadows et al. 2004). Nevertheless, these stand in
striking contrast to simulations and modeling premised on complexity, for
example, those models of change developed at the Sante Fe Institute for the
Future (although, as I argue in the next chapter, these exercises in "unpre-
dictability" are only too predictable). And, moreover, they hardly jive with
the actual track of what has been the field of "future studies" from the 1960s.

THE TURN TO FUTURE STUDIES

As futurists of all kinds are fond of saying, they do not offer predictions,
although a predictive dimension nevertheless uneasily coexists with a more
descriptive mission. One of the founding futurists, Jim Dator (1998: 4), explains: "Everyone agreed that future studies does not try to 'predict' the
future, in the sense of saying precisely what will happen to an individual,
organization or country before it actually happens. However, many of the
authors admit that they were originally drawn into futures in the hope that—
indeed, often in the firm belief that—it would be possible to predict the future if one just had the correct theory, methods, data, and, of course, enough
funding." Indeed, the discipline of "future studies" (with Master's granting
programs at University of Hawaii, University of Houston, and other places)
is much more involved with the elicitation and description of "alternative
futures," but the cachet of "futurist" still lies in the claim to exert some
control over the future. Again, Dator (1998: 4) writes: "Most futurists therefore *forecast* a wide variety of 'alternative futures' rather than predicting 'the
future.' They also seek to help people (students, clients community groups,

even entire nations) invent and try to move to their 'preferred future,' at the same time monitoring their progress towards it, and reconsidering their preference in the light of new information and experience gained as time goes by." But there is a lot of ambiguity in "invent," "forecast," and "monitor"; the role of the futurist in these formulations vacillates between the future conceived as something out there to be discovered and the future as the end product of deliberate intervention. It is in the interstices of this that anthropologists have most often intervened.

Several methodologies have been developed within the auspices of future studies that echo anthropological fieldwork techniques in interesting (and often unacknowledged) ways. Probably the most well known of these kinds of futurist projects are variants of what is called the "Delphi Method." Developed in 1964 at RAND, Delphi involves a tendentious succession of interviews with "experts" in science and policy. As Robert Lempert et al. (2003: 16) summarize, "In successive rounds, a group of experts is asked to supply responses to a list of questions. At the conclusion of every round, the participants view each other's answers and may change their views in light of what others believe. The answers are presented anonymously to eliminate the possibility that undue weight will be placed on the responses of persons who hold particular high statuses within the group." From these interviews stem a number of products. First, there are the initial interviews themselves, a polyphony of futures from the perspectives of different disciplines and different heuristics. However, this is only the starting point; Delphi continues on to the next round by requiring participants to review each other's responses, changing theirs in turn to craft a consensual vision of the future in what is designed as a self-fulfilling prophecy. That is, Delphi uses, essentially, the power of suggestion coupled with a kind of Milgram-esque manufacture of consent to produce a desired future state using informants who will be both the agents and beneficiaries of future change. Delphi in this respect is the exact opposite of a critical method; it actually serves to silence alternatives.

> In round one, Questionnaire 1 (Q1), the Delphi method presents an issue or states a problem in broad terms and then invites answers and comments/ The responses to Q1 are summarized and used to construct Questionnaire 2 (Q2)/ Q2 presents the results of Q1 and gives respondents an opportunity to re-evaluate their original answers in light of comprehensive feedback on the entire respondent group. ... This iterative process is continued until consensus or clear disagreement is reached among the panel. (Moldrup et al. 2002: 6)

In this formulation, the outliers are forced to concede to the tyranny of the majority; after all, like Bill Murray in *Groundhog Day,* Delphi panelists awaken each morning to an iteration of their future narratives until they finally leave hubris behind and fall in line with the will of the group. There have been several, interesting variants on Delphi since its introduction (for example, Foresight), but these still remain the methods of policy studies and marketing, with Delphi used to shape new products (Moldrup et al. 2002; Mullins 2006) or just to create consent within an institutional structure (Tatsuya et al. 2005).

The Delphi Method is probably best known through some of its popular variants, whereby magazines (Wired, et cetera) poll the experts, "Six Trends that Are Changing the World" (*Wired* 2006), about trends in technologies that are then adduced for their role in changing culture and society with, of course, the self-fulfilling goal of increasing attention on those selfsame technologies. Other well-known works—for example, John Naisbitt's *Megatrends* (1988)—dispense with the need for experts (other than its omniscient author), but still utilize a consensual vision of the future with the ultimate goal of catalyzing that future as much as predicting it. Thus, for Naisbitt (as well as for the Tofflers, George Gilder, Ray Kurzweil, and others), the goal of these intervention-predictions is to specify which technologies or economic shifts will arise, manufacturing the need for social and cultural change on the tails of their prediction.

Even when futurists (and, again, it is certainly a mistake to lump them all together like this) look to the cultural future, à la Alvin and Heidi Toffler, it is not exactly with an eye toward novelty and surprise. The Toffler's oeuvre, built on the idea of sweeping, global change impacting every element of life from corporations and democracy to leisure and identity, is still premised on technological change, but these "waves" are much more sweeping and totalizing. While Michael Marien, for example, in a snarling review of the Toffler's most recent submission, *Revolutionary Wealth,* takes great umbrage at their recapitulated characterization of our future as culminating in a post-industrial "third-wave," it is only because Marien himself has already hypothesized a "fourth-wave" upon which we are now entering (Marien 2006).

But this demonstrates the assumptions in these kinds of trends- or scenarios-elicitation methods. The emphasis on technologies, et cetera, is not only an artifact of the assumptions of futurists and their clients (many of whom work in emerging technologies markets), but it also subordinates "culture" to a kind of precipitate of technological change, a form of simplistic determinism which, while popular in 1970s-era materialism (see Harris 1974), has been rejected by otherwise materialist-oriented anthropologists (Nazarea 1998). Of course, if you're building your empire speaking at business conventions like George Gilder, you had better focus on the "next technological thing"; only through hyping accelerating IT can you capture the imagination of CEOs. But is this really imagination? As Gilder (2006) writes in a recent *Wired* article, "Moore's law has a corollary that bears the name of Gordon Bell, the legendary engineer behind Digital Equipment's VAX line of advanced computers and now a principal researcher at Microsoft. According to Bell's law, every decade a new class of computer emerges from a hundredfold drop in the price of processing power. As we approach a billionth of a cent per byte of storage, and pennies per gigabit per second of bandwidth, what kind of machine labors to be born?" That is to say, the question for the futurist here is not really future speculation, but future algebra; what will computers look like in ten years? How can those forecasts be capitalized on to reap value? Let's do the math! The continuation of the institutions and social relations attributed to the "New Economy" remain inviolate. In other words, the "futures" promulgated looks remarkably similar across the globe—globalization already a fait accompli in these theorists' minds. The future, for Gilder, is always already safely tucked away into corporate campuses in North California, Oregon, and Washington. That is, technologies will dizzyingly spiral intro the stratosphere, but the social structures that enfold them will, apparently, remain the same. "We" will live forever, according to Ray Kurzweil (2006), and hyperbolic technologies will enable us to realize all of our dreams, but, thankfully, it still looks like IT professionals will be drinking Starbucks in their suburban shopping centers. In Gilder's vision, corporate CEOs can breathe a sigh of relief: the future will be "manned" by white people.

This has been the primary complaint of people writing in the still-nascent movement of "Afro-Futurism."[1] Confronted with "waves" of futurist prognostications that, literally, engulf the racial and class Other in a tsunami of global capitalism, people on the passive end of these rapidly techno-utopian scenarios have no choice but to attempt to create a space for their own, more autonomous future imaginings. As Kodwo Eshun (2003: 292) explains of neo-liberal forecasting for Africa,

> These powerful descriptions of the future demoralize us; they command us to bury our heads in our hands, to groan with sadness. Commissioned by multinationals and nongovernmental organizations (NGOs), these developmental futurisms function as the other side of the corporate utopias that make the future safe for industry. Here, we are seduced not by smiling faces staring brightly into a screen; rather, we are menaced by predatory futures that insist the next 50 years will be hostile.
>
> Within an economy that runs on SF capital and market futurism, Africa is always the zone of the absolute dystopia. There is always a reliable trade in market projections for Africa's socioeconomic crises. Market dystopias aim to warn against predatory futures, but always do so in a discourse that aspires to unchallengeable certainty.

This goes far beyond realistic understandings of the many challenges African peoples face today; it extends to a way of representing "Africa" as a place somehow ancillary to the future. That is, in the framework of the World Trade Organization and the International Monetary Fund, there is little to be hopeful about in an Africa torn by war and disease. But not only this: in the projections of futurists, there is no Africa; that is, "waves" and "trends" elide the continent altogether, colonizing the language of the future for the West. The only hope for these places, in the terms of nineteenth-century anthropology, is to accede to Europe's past, a Horatio Alger discourse that only colonials could manage to believe.

Of course, many in the futures field have themselves critiqued the Eurocentric pretensions of future studies. In "Occupied Territory," Patricia Kelly (2002: 561) outlines the assumptions that overdetermine a Western, global future:

1. The only worldview, and the associated metaphysics and values, worthy of attention is the *Western* civilization's worldview;
2. There is only one science of nature, that is objective, positivist and universal,
3. "Reality," however it is defined, is constructed in the image of the white man;
4. Cultural difference will fade away as people discover the superiority of rational *Western* culture.

This, despite a robust growth over the last decades in Afrofuturism and indigenous futures that contest a future centered on the West and on a linear, European line of development. Can we think about Dine people on Mars (*The 6th World*)? Or a future Toronto as a First Nations space (*Biidaaban*) (Lempert 2018). Can we really think of these as Dine or Anishinaabe, or are "we" simply slotting people into settler ideologies about the future? Here, anthropology has been as guilty as any, with an emphasis on an ethnographic present that suspends people in a "contemporary" that is already a historical diorama of life as soon as it is published. In these textual strategies, "the future" will always be retrograde. This leads up, as Escobar writes, to "the effacement of entire worlds through a set of epistemological operations concerning knowledge, time, productivity, and ways of thinking about scale and difference" (Escobar 2017: 68).

ON TO CULTURAL FUTURES

It is in this context—an already attenuated future—that anthropologists first encounter futures studies in the late 1960s, and this very much despite Mead's insistence on an "open future." The first, official entrée of futures studies into anthropology, however, had to wait until the 1970s, when Arthur Harkins and Magoroh Maruyama organized an American Anthropological Association Symposium. The call for papers for the 1973 symposium suggests the very different grounds from which anthropologists were working (Harkins and Maruyama 1973: 32): "Commonly, culture change is considered to result from technological development. Can we reverse the trend and generate cultural goals ahead of technology, and make technology serve the generated cultural goals? How can cultural goals be generated from grass-roots up, instead of from top-down?" Harkins and Maruyama directly elaborate on the Mead-ian legacy. As the apical ancestor for futures studies in anthropology, it is no mistake that she contributes the introductory essay to their *Cultures of the Future* (1978). Accordingly, their work suffers from some of the same sorts of ambiguities as Mead. For example, it's unclear here what exactly would constitute a "cultural goal" (what is the "goal" of something like culture?), and also disheartening to see "culture" and "technologies" relegated—as they are in so much of Western discourse—to separate moieties. And there's the emphasis on engineering, the "cultural tinkering" that future-oriented anthropologists have always assumed would be anthropology's contribution, despite the ethical scandals that have erupted whenever anthropologists try to direct the course of culture change (Borofsky 2005). But what we do see here is an attempt to forge a place for anthropological discourse on the future, one centered on culture, rather than technology, and cultures, rather than one, myopic *Star Trek* culture stretching to infinity. This was the genesis of futures studies in anthropology.

Reed Riner (1987: 314)—another founder of future studies in anthropology—suggests that anthropology contributes to two, wide areas—policy-driven studies, on the one hand, and more light-hearted speculation, on the other: "Their interests are expressed in the other portions of anthropological futures literature which includes cross-cultural comparison of space-time conceptualizations, structural and semantic analyses of popular images of the future, and studies of hypothetical or idea experiments represented by actual international community experiments and the imagined space-habitat and culture contact simulations of the annual CONTACT conferences." It was Maruyama's more policy-oriented futures-work that seems, however, to have survived into successive American Anthropological Association conferences; indeed, Maruyama's prolific work seems to have outpaced anthropology altogether, and he was soon writing in the more instrumental, futuristic circles. He is remembered today primarily as a futurist and systems theorist (Caley 1994).

The more ludic, speculative dimension of "cultural futuristics" coalesced in *Cultural Futures Research,* itself a combination of two earlier periodicals, *ANTHRO-TECH: A Journal of Speculative Anthropology* (1976–1982) and *Cul-*

tural and Education Futures (1979–1982). CFR's editor, Reed Riner (1982: 3), stressed the interdisciplinary quality of the journal, which, he believed, answered the need to foster increased dialogue among social scientists, futurists, and science fiction writers/users, "cognizant that we are all educators." Indeed, articles during the journal's two-year run (1982–1984) included applied anthropology, cultural studies of then-emergent information technologies and regular contributions from science fiction novelist, M. A. Foster.

But there were shortcomings to this florescence of cultural futures as well. In 1973, Harkins and Maruyama held a contest for fictional accounts of "cultural alternatives." The winning papers demonstrate, perhaps, the limits of the anthropological imagination. Dorothy L. Keur's and Russel La Due's "Univaria" is a case in point: a utopian Great Society with technological fixes and a benevolent (yet menacing), Keynesian state solving all social problems. The mise-en-scene for this "alternative future" is a history classroom in the twenty-first century, where children and their teacher compare their present to a gravely flawed past. Precociously bright, futuristic middle-school students lead the discussion. "Kurt" begins:

> "Everyone in Univaria can be sure of a living wage. Those who lose their jobs, or are for any reason out of work, still get that basic unit of income. In the late twentieth century it would have been about $5000 per year."
>
> "But not like what they used to call welfare," said Ruth, breaking into the discussion for the first time. "Everyone gets it, but they have to work for it. On whatever government project is in progress nearby."
>
> "And if they refuse?" asked the teacher.
>
> "No one has refused," Ruth answered. "But if they do, the law says they will be deported. We have this arrangement with several of the undeveloped countries to accept our citizens."(Keur and La Due 1978: 597–598)

H. L. Lefferts (1978: 630) actually introduced this story into his anthropology classroom and reports that students found it, predictably, "old" and "dull," and, interestingly, "ethnocentric," that is, premised on US-style apotheoses of technocratic progress, free-market individualism, and the role of the State. Having unleashed their imaginations in the creation of "new patterns of living," those "new patterns," unfortunately, turn out to be pale evocations of one, myopic vision of the present. It is hardly reassuring that academics who spend their lives studying cultural alterity can only come up with a particularly Orwellian version of the Keynesian state.

But is this the only option? Does futures research in anthropology only depend upon the strained imagination of anthropologists; are anthropologists just so many more futurists pushing their own suspect scenarios? Luckily, no. In the 1970s, following on the tails of the AAA cultural futuristics symposia, Robert Textor took a sabbatical to begin reading about the nascent field of cultural futures, from which he developed his own methodological variant, Ethnographic Futures Research (EFR), as an antidote to the "tempocentrism" he saw around him; that is, "to one's being unduly centered in one's own temporality" (Textor 2003: 522). This "tempocentrism" was more than just a lack of imagination, it actually had (and has) serious consequences—in, for example, monolithic schemes of development that hinge upon technology transfer of a "miraculous" technology: the "miracle rice" of the Green Revolution and the GMO wheat and soy of today.[2] In this insidious replacement of biodiversity with monocropping on a huge scale, we are only beginning to understand the consequences of this limited horizon of "futures thinking" (Hess and Hess 2000). Instead, EFR promised to elaborate on alternatives to monolithic schemes of development: "Moreover, I saw a great opportunity for anthropologists to enhance and improve research on alternative futures for people indigenous to the non-Western world. Although the great majority of social scientists in the world, of whatever discipline, are Westerners, cultural anthropology is unique among disciplines in virtually requiring that its members at least try to develop sophisticated and empathic understandings of non-Western peoples" (Textor 2005: 24–25). Textor's method bears similarities to the Delphi Method of the 1960s—interviews with people designed to elaborate futures along a range of preferability. And yet, there are substantial differences. For one thing, the Delphi Method narrows down the possibilities to a manageable few using a succession of questionnaires. In fact, Lempert et al (2004: 18) complain that "the method errs when it encourages experts to reach consensus on the latter rather than articulate the former." Delphi has developed into a management tool; it is not a method for examining cultural alternatives, but for winnowing down the alternatives to the future in order to engineer a predictable (profitable, efficient) future for the organization. Textor's method focuses on the expansion of alternatives; the point is to generate alternatives themselves: "The method I developed, known as Ethnographic Futures Research (EFR), builds upon one's ethnographic knowledge, but systematically asks questions about the future. The EFR interview has much in common with the ethnographic interview. It is confidential, interactive, semi-structured, flexible, open-ended, and focused on patterns and systems" (Textor 2005: 25). That is, instead of asking respondents to select from a finite set of already structured futures—as in Delphi—EFR doesn't initially beg the question of what exactly the "future" might be. Although, there is still structure; Textor (25) asks informants to imagine "an Optimistic, a Pessimistic, and a Most Probable scenario."

The tour de force of Textor's method is *The Middle Path for the Future of Thailand* (1990), a collaborative work applying EFR to a physicist and public figure in Thailand; in fact, the book is credited to Sippanondha Ketudat himself, with Textor listed as providing "methodological and editorial consultation." That is, Textor has used EFR to facilitate Dr. Sippanondha's articulation of his own future:

> To supply a framework for elicitation, I asked Dr. Sippanondha to imagine a continuum of 100 possible future sociocultural systems for Thailand as a time-horizon of his own choosing, which turned out to be the year 2563 of the Buddhist era, or AD 2020. Moving from the left pole to the right, there will be, in theory, 100 positions on this continuum. Position number 1, located at the left pole, was dubbed by his values as the worst possible sociocultural future for Thailand, while position number 10, at the right pole, was defined as the best possible. Futures located farther right (more desirable) than 100 were defined as utopian and impossible. Futures located farther left (less desirable) than 1 were defined as dystopian and, likewise, improbable. (Textor 1995: 463)

Of course, this is not just Dr. Sippanondha opining in a vacuum; Textor has already structured the sorts of narratives Sippanondha will produce with the unmistakable impress of Enlightenment discourse, and while there's certainly value in stipulating that Sippanondha consider "utopian" or "dystopian" futures as asymptotes in terms of his own speculations, it may be that "utopia" and "dystopia" are not really appropriate genres for talking of Thai futures at all. Nevertheless, it is entirely appropriate for the informant, a physicist with experience in policy as equally comfortable in rural Thailand as in more putatively global contexts.

And what Sippanondha articulates is in many ways profoundly different from the monolithic discourse on the future as the acceleration of invention and the homogenization of culture. Instead, Sippanondha (1990: 128–129) suggests a future where Thailand reigns in the power of technology and modernization in particularly Thai ways:

> A salient traditional Thai characteristic is generalized empathic kindness (*namcaj*). That Thai morpheme *caj*, which may be roughly translated as "heart," is found in well over 300 Thai terms. This is a truly remarkable pattern, and suggests to me at least, that the notion of heart, feeling and empathic concern is pervasive in our culture. And that "caring heart" can legitimately be considered a basic aspect of Thai identity. I am projecting optimistically—and indeed most probably—that this feature of our culture and identity will survive essentially intact.

And even more than this—against Thai culture as a kind of "survival" amidst modern institutions and modernizations—he is optimistic that "progress" will mean not only a more modern, more prosperous Thailand, but more perfect realizations of Thai identity: "Optimistically, a pattern will become increasingly prevalent in which running a company "according to the Dharma" of Buddhism (or the ethical code of some other great religion), will serve to promote an equitable sharing of the fruits of annual gains in productivity" (85). That is, capitalism will develop into a Buddhist future (rather than Buddhism being conceived as some kind of blockade to the "free market"). That is reserved for his "Pessimistic" scenarios, which, unfortunately, have come to pass in the form of International Monetary Fund–mandated restructuring after the crash of the Baht in 1997. But what's interesting here is that Sippanondha is free to imagine all of these futures without necessarily conforming to the singular future plied by the futurists: more capitalism, faster technologies, more profit, more productivity, more money. That he still envisions increased technological productivity is a testament not only to his background as scientist and technocrat, but also to his hope that Thailand twenty-five years in the future will command global prominence (but not, importantly, global hegemony).

It is not too much to suggest that Ethnographic Futures Research has the effect of not only helping people in other places to imagine non-Western futures, but can also serve as a corrective to unilinear conceptions of Western futures. As Riner (1991: 307) suggests, "Ethnographic futures research enables us to apprehend and clarify what our hosts, informants, and/or clients envision about the future, to reconstruct a lexicon of their expectations or a grammar of their hopes and fears, to discover and make explicit the hidden premises and indigenous process rules, about the future as these are entertained and as they may be shared among members of a group or organization where policies or strategies are formulated or implemented." Thus, EFR can simultaneously liberate *and* critique, evoke a certain vision of the future while providing a sort of critical perspective from which to reflect.

This is what Reed Riner has done in his Solar System Simulation (SolSys), which asks students to design future extraplanetary colonizations based on their own vision of a "probable" future fifty to one hundred years hence and then, heir to early computer games, act out those futures online in a multiuser dungeon (MUD). As Riner and Jennifer Clodius (1995: 98) explain:

> Third, we stimulate students to think in multiple future tenses. In each iteration, the students have decided that the first permanent settlement on Mars could feasibly be in the mid-2070s. From that date they look back to the present and "reconstruct" the events that led up to their situation; this entails thinking holistically about all of Earth's sociocultural systems. And they look ahead to the future of their settlement; this entails sensitive consideration of the continuity of past, through present, with future. Thinking systematically about alternative, plausible futures has a strong impact on all of one's thinking.... Thinking in a future context, as our students do, adds a second tense to futures thinking, with additional general "consciousness raising," but as yet unspecified, impacts on their cognitive structures.

I can personally attest to what those "unspecified impacts" might be through my own four-year involvement with SolSys. Having students formulate "plausible futures" for the simulation is not exactly a mind-expanding experience. Student futures invariably involve a succession of world wars, ecological disasters, SF-inflected inventions: in short, the dreck of decades of Hollywood science fiction. More than simply recycling shop-worn themes, however, these images actively re-inscribe the present into the future: thus, students invariably see the future as shaped through the geopolitical struggle of super powers, with China taking the place of the Soviet Union. They invariably see the colonization of Mars as the expansion of capitalism in extraplanetary space, with technologies catalyzing the formation of a more militaristic society.

The temptation would be to see this as a failure on the part of students' imaginations. While certainly not representing a high-water mark of imaginative thinking, what I've used SolSys for is as a tool for critiquing the "consensual" future, where the language of the future is already colonized by the present, where, as Shari Popen (2002: 390–391) complains, we live "in the midst of a totalizing culture that produces and contains our capacity to engage in substantive critique." That is, the most egregious error in these futures is not so much that they are derived from countless other narratives of interplanetary battles and ecological apocalypse, but that they, as Kim Stanley Robinson points out, "portray the current triumph of capitalism as inevitable, eternal, and unbeatable" (Szeman and Whiteman 2004: 186). In the classroom, reflecting on the sheer banality of these manufactured futures stimulates students not so much to imagine alternatives as admit the need for imagined alternatives, or, as Fredric Jameson (2005: 416) writes, not the "presentation of radical alternatives," but "simply the imperative to imagine them." What these futures show is the assumptions people bring to the future—the future as the battle for national hegemony (the future as the US Future), the progress of technology, the continuation of a status quo politics vacillating between moderate and radical conservatism, the endless continuation of capitalism. But it does more In addition, EFR breaks us out of thinking in terms of singular futures. This is what Riner does in his "Flagstaff Tomorrow" project, articulating the futures thinking of ordinary residents along with experts (Riner 1998).

Games and simulations have continued as a source of critique as well as a source of critical alternatives, although they, like other examples of mass culture, can be strongly reactionary (Collins 2020). One example: the game *The Thing From the Future* (Situation Labs, 2017) asks players to design and present theoretical artifacts from the future that reflect prompts taken from randomly dealt cards. What the game tends to solicit are some stereotypical utopian or dystopian future scenarios, although there are other possibilities as well, depending on the cards. For example, the "transform" card can be combined with a variety of nontechnological "terrain" cards (e.g., "socialism," "home") to at least suggest alternative possibilities to the usual linearity and ethnocentrism of the Western development narrative. Other simulations are similarly ambiguous, and, like anthropology, can be used to stimulate alternative possibilities or to simply legitimate the present. While academics and designers like Elizabeth LaPensée have devised games that have challenged the obdurate linearity of Western modernity, science fiction continues to buttress racial hierarchies, with, for example, much of "cyberpunk" simply recapitulating nineteenth- and early twentieth-century "yellow peril" narratives for dystopian evocations of white decline (Chan 2020).

In any case, the spike in anthropology conference papers and publications devoted to "the future" had subsided by the 1990s, a product, perhaps, of a precipitous decline in anthropology enrollments, funding for anthropology programs, and a panicked surge in "vocomania," the overwhelming preference for education legitimated by neoliberal governance.

The reluctance of anthropologists, in general, to prognosticate can also be traced to the 1980s critique of materialist, "cybernetic" models of human behavior and, as a corollary, the growing skepticism that anthropology could proffer a "true" representation of empirical reality. In addition, there were sustained, damning critiques of development and the sorts of remedial prognostication implied in discourses on modernization (Escobar 1995). Quite rightly, anthropologists began distancing themselves from discourses on the future so thoroughly penetrated by specious "orientalisms" and totalizing discourses arrogantly derogating non-Western institutions to the dustbins of underdevelopment. For anthropologists, the "crisis of representation" that cast doubt on our ability to say what *is* had the effect of limiting what anthropologists said *could be*. "On the one hand we take pride in expert knowledge, relative to others, of social form and the likely outcome of social process; on the other, we are nervous of anything that smacks of prediction" (Wallmann 1992: 1).

The other option is to let the "native" prognosticate, that is, to bow out of a process that might be said to be thoroughly suspect in a post-Enlightenment era. This might involve, as Victoria Razak suggests, leaving the putative "future" behind in the course of teasing out indigenous alternatives. In other words, what anthropologists are looking for may not be identified as "the future" at all, since this already begs the questions of linear development, progress, and Western-style teleologies. As Razak (1996: 648) writes,

Islanders look forwards and backwards in the creation of culture. Symbols are those jettisoned from the past based on their facility to protect and maintain valued aspects of extant culture and are sometimes intermixed with the orienting symbols of specific desired futures. Mapping this (essentially political) process of symbolic development over time can suggest alternative images of possible culture futures in the same way that a symbolic archaeology of the past reveals the so-called classic periods of earlier societies through unearthing and interpreting their cultural material.

This has more in common with Ernst Bloch's everyday utopics, where there lies "a Utopian impulse governing everything future-oriented in life and culture, and encompassing everything from games to patent medicines, from myths to mass entertainment, from iconography to technology, from architecture to eros, from tourism to jokes and the unconscious" (Jameson 2005: 2). In the work of indigenous persons, the question is not which future to elaborate, but to have a "future" on their own terms at all, where the future has been tendentiously operationalized as (1) assimilationist (everyone moving simultaneously towards European-style hyper-modernity, and (2) "traditional," that is, indigenous peoples surviving into the future as relics of the past. The "future" is European and American, maybe Japanese, but never centered on indigenous people. Even when the State officially adopts a "multicultural" future, it is one where indigenous identities form the "survivals" in a globalizing world, barely tolerated for the tourist revenue they contribute. As Faye Ginsburg and Fred Myers (2006: 29) complain of multicultural policy in Australia, "Where, in all this debate, are the people with whom we have been working over the last two decades—the painters, the musicians, the media makers—in short, the cultural activists who are shaping, through their cultural labor, possibilities for Aboriginal futures outside the defining limits of law and policy?" That is, there is nothing in official futures for the "modern" Aboriginal and, even more so, no acknowledgement that the media makers, writers and artists themselves may transform the State, thus forge an aboriginal future for Australia, rather than simply subsist on the receiving of end of State policy—whether beneficent or belligerent. Against these powerful (mis)representations, Ginsberg, Myers, and others engaged in "indigenous media" have used their advocacy to catalyze alternative representations, "developing a counter discursive Aboriginal imaginary that is crucial to their contemporary self-production and the creation of a 'cultural future'" (Ginsburg and Myers 2006: 29).

The real "alternative" future is not marked as such; it will require the work of an anthropologist, a utopian, and a dialectician to bring it into the futurist light, but even this has its dangers; in the act of articulating these "futures" for an audience largely embedded in Spencerian progress, what gets left behind? The minutiae of everyday life? Here is where anthropological representation makes a great deal of difference. Instead of incorporating Other futures into our own, dominant discourse, "we can participate in understanding and amplifying their projects of cultural creativity that go far beyond mere survival, drawing attention to the possibilities of the creation of culture as an ongoing emancipatory project" (Ginsburg and Myers 2006: 43).

Perhaps the best role of the anthropologist might be the articulation of alternative stories, rather than adding our own mediocre narratives. As Razak and Sam Cole (1995: 376) suggest, "If *the future* is beyond our ken, then why not dispense with ersatz probability and generate multiple potential futures: we 'try out' alternative boundaries, create overshoot conditions. Our only limit, beyond our creative capacity, is that these stories of possible futures must, like any good story, hang together in basic details, basic conceptions. At least we are creating a space in which to think."

With the renewed popularity of "the future" in anthropology, we see a variety of (sometimes oblique) engagements with themes in futurology, some of them linked to the developing alternative ways of life to the environmentally disastrous consumer capitalism that exercises absolute hegemony in impoverished narratives of Western futures. For example, Biehl and Locke emphasize an "unfinished" future where anthropologists cultivate "a conscientious empiricism wedded to a radical analytical openness to complexity and wonder" (Biehl and Locke 2017a: xi). Here, the "futurology" revolves around moments when the "partial"—the emergent, the submerged—might be evoked to help us envision alterative futures and "restore our capacity to perceive the becomings of our subjects, even amid dire situations and against darkening political horizons" (Biehl and Locke 2017b: 21). Here, anthropology discards the predictive for the evocative, teasing at the alternative, shadowy possibilities eclipsed by the linearity of neoliberal futures.

NOTES

Parts of this chapter have been previously published as "Sail On! Sail On! Anthropology, Science Fiction and the Enticing Future," *Science Fiction Studies* 30(2) (2003): 180–98. The author would like to thank the publication for permission to use the material here.

1. There are several authoritative histories of Afrofuturism, including accounts that locate the beginning of the movement in the SF of W. E. B. Du Bois, among others (Womack 2013; Anderson and Jones 2015).
2. These technology transfer schemes are the heirs to the Victorian Time Machine, e.g., by promising that GMO products will wrench the "undeveloped" world into "our" time.

Chapter 6

The Surprising Future

There is little need to advocate for this or that futurist methodology in areas of emergent information and biotechnology. Instead, the future seems to crowd into the present, with insights into the human genome disclosing futures suddenly no longer merely immanent, but fully realized; futuristic films dramatizing eugenics (*Gattica*) or intelligent agents (*I, Robot*) seem curiously dated in this technological surfeit, and scholars in Science and Technology Studies have turned their attention to the attendant social and cultural contexts that, like their material counterparts, seem to leap out of the future. This emphasis on what Michael Fischer (2003) terms "prolepsis" shifts attention away from the "present" to the "future-in-the-present," that is, the emergent, those shadowy cultural practices, identities, and relationships in the process of becoming, one leg barely visible in unstable assemblages in the present, the other hidden away within the penumbra of the future. In the tradition of cultural studies of science, we have appropriated many of our ideas of the emergent from the "science of complexity" (for example, strains of research in the life sciences, systems theory, and the computer sciences) and made them speak to culture, power, and emancipatory possibility. In a politically quiescent time (in the US, at least), this is good strategy; identifying sites of hybridity is one step on a road to more concerted resistance, and what better discipline than anthropology to identify the forgotten, marginalized, and repressed meanings and practices, and then intervene in their revelation?

Ironically, emergent anthropologies—anthropology's speculative investments in cultural futures—are oftentimes merely dull, recapitulations of the past. In a recent collection, *Histories of the Future,* anthropologists train their gaze on sites of the future in California and the West. As Daniel Rosenberg and Susan Harding (2005: 13) write, "this region became a laboratory, an imaginary, in which we explored the cultural and sentimental microdynamics of future making." And yet, these anthropologies of the emergent not only recapitulate previous anthropological encounters with the future (for example, Mead 2005), but also evoke futures that have already become part of the past. For example, Harding (9) cautions readers that this collection is designed as a "hypertext, opening up analytic paths among disparate temporal experiences of modernity." But, of course, it is not. But in the 1980s, comp-utopian prognostications predicted that academic publishing would move to online, densely networked texts fenestrated in a continuously expanding webs of signification.[1] Although ebook versions of the book exist, they are—with few exceptions—self-contained. Yes, hyperlinks can be (and are) added to ebooks, but in reality they are almost never added, contrary to compu-utopian prognostications that predicted academic publishing would move to texts densely networked to each other through a Berners-Lee-esque decoupage of hyperlinks. The reason for this is, of course, that capitalism is inimical to the untrammeled flow of information—the "knowledge economy" is much more about the commodification of knowledge than its free flow, and that "free," finally, is itself fraught with power and contradiction (Collins 2009). But *Histories of the Future* is only one example; all of us risk bathos when we evoke the emergent. What counts as "emergent" may prove to have already emerged; novelty may well prove derivative, revolutionary may be subverted back into the status quo, in an appropriately derivative fashion, first as tragedy, second as farce, and third as tragic nostalgia for farce.[2]

The following chapter looks to anthropological appropriations of "emergence" from multiagent systems research and the sciences of complexity and argues that emergence, in anthropological discourse, occupies an ambiguous position. On the one hand, ideas of emergence offer anthropologists access to novelty, that is, not only a perspective on the production of new cultural assemblages, but their transcendent power, what Jane Bennett (2001: 98) describes (qua the magic of Paraclesus) as the "morphing transformation from one state, space or form to another." That is, "emergence" offers anthropologists a new lien on the "ethnographer's magic," a different sleight-of-hand that opens a window on the future through our ethnographies of the present. However, it's worth interrogating these new anthro-myths of transcendence. Why, we might ask, have anthropologists begun appropriating a discourse that itself—having crested in popularity in the 1980s—is no longer particularly new and that has already been readily appropriated by New Economy management gurus? Much of this can be explained by shifts in what might be termed, after Harold Bloom, anthropology's "anxiety of influence," where in more overtly imperial days anthropologists spoke of "their" tribe and "their" culture, protecting a monopoly over knowledge of the cultural other.[3] But in a complex society, anthropologists must abandon the "savage slot" for another strategic claim to expertise—future developments—

that, like knowledge of the "small society" in the first half of the twentieth century, is premised on a curious relationship with time. The "savage slot" depends upon relegating the Other to the past while an anthropology of the emergent places the source of cultural alterity into the future; in both cases, anthropology's truth claims depend upon a privileged relationship to these different times. But as with the "savage slot," "emergence" may act as a screen under which recidivist ideas about identity, progress, and power can continue under the sigil of the new, conceived here not as break with the past but as what Walter Benjamin describes as a "Hell" of the new. But by appropriating the notion of "surprise" from multiagent systems research, I try to reclaim the potential of emergence to gesture toward a transformative anthropology.

EMERGENCE MERGING

To begin with, "emergence" itself is an emergent concept—that is to say, its present meaning seems irreducible to past usages. Michael Fischer (2003: 56) outlines two strikingly different meanings: "First is the organizational concept that relations among physics, chemistry, and biology are 'levels of organization' that emerged through evolution.... A second, if related, notion of 'emergence' is that of contested 'emergent forms of life,' the continued renegotiation of historical and emergent modalities of ethical and political reason." On the one hand, something is said to emerge when we cannot derive it from the properties of its constituents components; for example, until the advent of quantum-level explanations, "water" was said to be emergent from hydrogen and oxygen, that is to say, the properties of water were irreducible to its supervenient parts (Sawyer 2001). On the other hand, "emergence" has been used to describe something not yet fully formed nor predictable. Anthropological formulations of the emergent flit between these.

In anthropology, "language," "civilization," and "culture" are all phenomena that have been said to "emerge" over the course of human evolution. These are often said to combine into an alchemist's blend of cultural, physical, and physiological change added to the alembic of the species in undetermined amounts. For example, in "Culture Matters in a Neolithic Transition and Emergence of Hierarchy in Thy, Denmark," Timothy Earle (2004: 111) looks to the "emergence of hierarchical social structures that followed the domestication plants and animals in the Neolithic," while Matthew Bandy (2004: 322) hypothesizes that "village fissioning will cease with the emergence of higher-level institutions." Both of these join countless, earlier works in cultural evolution that, with variations, look to the succession of the "simpler" by the more "complex" (or more "differentiated"). And yet, ineluctable as these evolutionary lineages may be, there's nevertheless a perfunctory sense that comes from the subterranean addition of historical time to the abyssal, synchronic stretch of cultural evolutionary time—more like a phase state. It reminds us that, to the Social Darwinist, the ladder goes both ways—"evolution" may reverse in "devolution" and, in the sense of Spengler, empires may rise or fall.

With "social facts," we can see an isomorphic variant of these usages. In fact, Keith Sawyer (2001, 2002) has attempted to reinvent Durkheim as an emergence theorist, with "social facts, collective representations, social currents, dynamic density, social milieu, social substratum, and *sui generis*" (2002: 232) as emergent properties irreducible to psychology, on the one hand, and material life, on the other. Critiquing other "emergence theorists" (this designation is also emergent in Sawyer's work), Sawyer (2002: 579) defines the work of emergence in sociology as a "nonreductive materialism—the position that mental properties are supervenient on the physical brain and yet not reducible to physical properties." Not only are they irreducible, but they additionally exert some influence over the disjunctive, atomistic elements from which they are (emergently) constituted. Thus, Durkheim's social fact is also causal, not simply the epiphenomena of more deterministic, more basic elements (232).

Both of these usages, however, seem strikingly different from contemporary operationalizations in that the social and cultural processes that are said to be emerging are already a fait accompli: language, social facts, culture, tool-making, and civilization are already constituted objects. The question for these "emergence theorists," to borrow Sawyer's designation, is the black box machinations that lead from physiological, psychological, and material inputs to these outputs. That is, they describe linear processes: nineteenth-century cultural evolutionism has been called "unilinear" because there is no question of what "emerges"; later iterations of cultural evolutionisms may have minimized the moral imperative of these kind of just-so etiologies, but the point is still to render casuistries for the present.

In contrast, much of the emergence in anthropology today indulges in the play of nonlinearity, that is, it is precisely the unknown which draws anthropologists to study cultural politics in the age of New Reproductive Technologies, or capital in the era of the mapped (and patented) genome. Rather than track the morphogenesis of cultural and social patterns (reductively selected, it must be said, from an infinitude of other forms, institutions, behaviors, and ideas as somehow primary), this "emergence" seems closer to Deleuze's sense of assemblage, a provisional, shadowy, outline of practices, institutions and identities that may or may not coalesce into something more solid. For example, Brian Keith Axel (2004: 26) suggests that "the fleeting emergence of an enunciative subject of diaspora within a single poetic performance compels an examination of the impact of violence and gender normativity for those who self-identify as Sikhs," while Cecilia McCallum (2005: 100) purports to "trace the emergence of racialization from residents' microhistorical passages through the metropolis as these sediment into a shared, if partial, knowledge about difference and identity." In these instances, "emergent" cultures form a virtual particle in the physics of culture.

This form of emergence owes it animus to what have been called the "sciences of complexity," isomorphic developments in the biological and computer sciences in the 1970s. Taking cues from Artificial Life and systems theory, anthropologists studying emergence train their methods on partial worlds in becoming, representing a remarkable departure from anthropology as a discipline with one foot in history (à la Kroeber). It betrays a longing among anthropologists for the novel, along with an uneasiness, perhaps, that an anthropology with one foot in history would be superseded in the hyper-acceleration of post-Fordist temporalities.

BUILDING FROM THE BOTTOM: GROWING COMPLEXITY

Apocryphally, 1950s Artificial Intelligence (AI) research foundered on its simplistic equation of computers, information processing, and intelligence, each of which, with the help of that philosopher's stone, information, could be transformed—at least in the dreams of Claude Shannon—into the other. Although reductive, cybernetics, as N. Katherine Hayles (1999) and others have demonstrated, is more complex than that, and much recent scholarship has focused on, for example, the Josiah Macy Conferences as sites of contestation, with Gregory Bateson, Margaret Mead, and William MacKay proposing variously embodied theories of information systems (Collins 2005b).

Less linear models succeeded the "brain-as-computer" model; some, rather than emulate human cognition, proposed beginning at the putative "bottom" of intelligence. As Johnston (2002: 493) summarizes: "In contrast, the new AI gives primary importance to 'bottom-up' processes by which intelligence emerges and evolves in biological life, particularly in interactions with the environment that enhances the agent's present situation and increases its chances for survival, or in which new kinds of organization and cooperation among multiple agents emerge." In mutltiagent systems, "agents" (human or non-human) interact with each other and the environment; compared to the agents envisioned in AI's "strong program," these agents, although autonomous, are considerably scaled down. Their "knowledge"—representations, drives, inborn schema, and so on—is incomplete, distributed across a population of agents who, while interacting, transcend the programming of any single agent. This interaction, or what Humberto Maturana and Francisco Varela term (in a slightly different context) "structural coupling," is said to be formative of new—emergent—cognition.

In some accounts of robotics, the shift from AI to various strands of mutltiagent systems begins with the work of Rodney Brooks (along with his coauthor, Anita Flynn). Their 1989 article, "Fast, Cheap and Out of Control," called for a complete rejection of the representational paradigm in AI for what they termed a "subsumption architecture." As they write of one of their early robot agents, "Nowhere in the control system is there any mention of a central controller calling these behaviors as subroutines. These processes exist independently, run at all times, and fire whenever the sensory preconditions are true" (1989: 481). That is, while the representational paradigm featured a "brain" composed of a model of the environment and a series of algorithms for navigating that environment, Brook's and Flynn's robots just *react,* replacing, as Brooks later described, a model based on an understanding of human cognition with one derived from ethology (Murphy 2000: 106). Each sensor/actuator acts independently of other sensor/actuators, but the resultant behavior—crawling, scuttling, et cetera—emerges out of the coordination of these independent, reactive drives. "But as the specific goals of the robot are never explicitly represented, nor are there any plans—the goals are implicit in the coupling of actions to perceptual conditions, and apparent execution of plans unroll in real time as one behavior alters the robot's configuration in the world in such a way that new perceptual conditions trigger the next sequence of actions" (Brooks 1997: 292). What was so striking about these 1980's and 1990's experiments in reactive architectures was not just the eerily animal-like movement of robots like Genghis (one of Brooks's prototypical, reactive robots), but their contingent quality. That is, Genghis's insect-like scuttlings are not programmed into the robot; instead, they emerge unexpectedly, surprising scientist and onlooker alike with their robot ethologies.

This is the biggest difference between this order of emergence and the more staid emergences in nineteenth and twentieth-century anthropology: its temporal contingency. What is emergent in multiagent systems unfolds along a temporality that cannot be predicted by any empirical accounting of the present. It is emergent precisely because it produces the unexpected. For multiagent systems theorists like Francisco Varela (1999: 17), it is this essential contingency that defines enaction (his own, influential theory of emergence): "Thus cognition consists not of representation but of *embodied action.* Thus we can say that the world we know is not pre-given; it is, rather, *enacted* through our history of structural coupling, and the temporal hinges that articulate enaction are rooted in the number of microworlds that are activated in every situation." In multiagent systems, Bergsonian emergence replaces Spencerian; from explaining the past, theorizing emergence shifts to anticipating a future. In science studies, Andrew Pickering (1995: 382) has termed this "the mangle," material and human agencies entangling in unexpected assemblages and resistances along a temporal axis. Unknown futures unfold, reconfiguring etiologies in the process. In Bergsonian emergence, "each form flows out of previous forms, while adding to them something new, and is explained by them as much as it explains them" (quoted in Ansell-Pearson 2002: 73).

We can see the difference in Marilyn Strathern's treatment of emergent kinship. Nineteenth-century anthropologists like Lewis Henry Morgan saw kinship as developing along specific teleologies (for example, savage to civilized). In contrast, Strathern starts from the growing incidence of multiple parentage in the context of new reproductive technologies; the challenges brought by people engaged in various forms of surrogacy over our ideological understandings of nucleated families together with the legal and scientific power wielded over the genome leads her back to reevaluate pivotal shifts in the eighteenth century in conceptions of family, kinship, authorship, and ownership, when both creative works and children could be thought of as "offspring" somehow related to their procreator. As she explains,

> Why this leap from one arena to another—from parental suits to scientific authorship? In each, debate turns on the implications of multiplicity. Yet surely we could not sustain an analogy long enough to think usefully about the former (parenthood) in terms of the latter (authorship)? The potential parallels can, therefore, be interesting for one reason only: because they bring to mind a possibility already realized, an occasion when someone has proffered connections of just this kind. I have not presented a work-out analogy between multiple parenthood and multiple authorship, but rather the kinds of raw materials from which such analogies are made and the cultural possibilities these contain: my pretend analogy sets the stage from one that was no pretense at all. (2002: 168–169)

When people argue in courts over who "owns" eggs and sperm, or who can exercise rights over children "multiply authored," these analogies—never more than suggestions—come again to the fore. Ultimately, of course, we do not treat children as economic property; nor, on the other hand, is knowledge (held in copyright) unambiguously "owned." Yet, genetic engineering and the emergent "genetic family" threaten to materialize an otherwise inchoate analogy (183): "A truism about knowledge can keep them in view: the genes that carry the data informing you of what you are at the very same time comprise the mechanisms about what you are. This looks like a reworking of an old theme, the constitutive nature of kinship knowledge. But to find kinship knowledge in the gene is, so to speak, to find it in itself. Knowledge and kinship become momentarily inseparable." This is a very different sort of mechanism than nineteenth-century emergence, where "the child is the father of the man," to use another kinship metaphor. Instead, Strathern describes phenomena that cannot be predicted, or, rather, that can only be "predicted" through a process of ex post facto redaction whereby future forms select their own past (conceived here as a "virtuality" actualized, à la Bergson and Deleuze).

But there's a missing element in contrasting these two forms of emergence; it is not enough to say that one works from the past to the present by delimiting the future while the other reworks the past and present by way of an open future. Instead, there's the element of novelty. Something emergent is not merely coincidentally surprising, it is precisely its unexpected appearance that causes anthropologists to label it in protean terms; no one, after all, can predict its final shape or import. What draws, for example, Stefan Helmreich (2001) to the cultural study of thermophilic microorganisms is not merely the possibility of new additions to Linnean taxonomies, but the promise (or the threat) of unsettling filiative classifications altogether, and in the process remake our understandings of other classes of filiation, including kinship and family.[4] In this sense of dislocating shock lies the power of emergence for anthropology; conversely, its lack signals a politically suspect, pseudo emergence. In order to understand how this process works, though, we should return to multiagent systems.

Peter Cariani is reported to have asked of A-Life scientists, "what distinguishes an emergent computation from an nonemergent one?" (Emmeche 1994: 149). If we take Andy Clark's (2001: 113–114) operating definitions of emergence as "unprogrammed functionality" or "interactive complexity," are there different degrees of emergence? For example, let's take a classic example of emergence in J. Hallam's and C. Malcolm's wall-following robot: "The robot follows walls encountered to the right by means of an in-built bias to move to the right, and a right-side sensor, contact activated, that causes it to veer slightly to the left. When these two biases are well calibrated, the robot follows the wall by a kind of 'veer and bounce' routine" (Clark 2001: 112). The observed behavior—following the wall—was never part of the robot's program, hence we might consider it an example of "unprogrammed functionality." And yet, what exactly, is emerging? There is nothing computationally emerging here—the same simple obstacle-avoidance subroutines are running; the "schema" (such as we can speak of one) is unchanged; the robot is utterly unaware of its novel behavior. So how can this robot's behavior be considered emergent?

For Peter Cariani (1991), emergence artificial in life simulations utilizing cellular automata or other nonlinear computational processes is an artifact of observation. Accordingly,

> emergence reveals itself as the behavioral deviation by the physical system from the observer's model of it. If we as observers look at a physical system that radically changes its inner structure, and thereby its behavior, we need to be able to observe the system's behavior (and eventually make predictions about it). If we can continue to track the system with the model we already have, then nothing essentially new has arisen in the system, and we will be unable to make any conclusions regarding emergence. (Emmeche 1994: 151)

If we consider the robot's behaviors according to the "computational machine states" we begin with (that is, the obstacle-avoidance subroutines), then there is no emergence. Only when we change the interpretative frame to include the wall do we get the sense of emergence. In the history of cybernetic systems, this is the classic problem of the observer, which Bateson, Mead, and others see contributing to what Katherine Hayles (1999) has termed the end of first-generation cybernetics and the beginning of the next, including Humberto Maturana's and Francisco Varela's theories of "autopoiesis." When we study a system, we have no choice but to study it from a perspective determinant in some respects. As Hayles (1999: 138–139) explains: "Here again the role of the observer becomes important, for Maturana is careful to distinguish between the triggering effect that event in a medium has on a system structurally coupled with it when they perceive the system interacting with the environment. When my dog sees a pigeon, I may think, 'Oh, he's pointing because he sees the bird.' But in Maturana's terms, this is an inference I draw in my position in the 'descriptive domain' of a human observer." It is easy to slip from this to an arid solipsism, but the intent of this second generation of cybernetic theorizing is to strengthen empiricism by including the position of the observer in the systems they describe (Varela 1999). For emergence, this is particularly important, since the phenomena would seem to depend both in the apperception and valuation of perceived behaviors. For example, the "V" shape formed by flocking birds is frequently adduced as an emergent phenomena: we cannot derive the ultimate shape of the flock from the individual birds themselves; the final shape combines instinct with aerodynamics. And yet, who is perceiving the "V" shape? Surely not the birds, each following the one in front. How, in other words, do observers decide whether or not a pattern or behavior counts as properly "emergent"? For Cariani, emergence is "able to set off emergent processes in our own minds" (Emmeche 1994: 153). But how does this take place? And isn't this just bracketing "emergence"?

In multiagent systems, researchers have utilized the idea of "surprise" for that moment when expected results contradict actual results. In their algebraic formulation, Edmund Ronald et al. (1999: 228) define the phenomena as when "the language of design *L1* and the language of observation *L2* are distinct, and the causal link between the elementary interactions programmed in *L1* and the behaviors observed in *L2* is *non-obvious* to the observer—who therefore experiences surprise." Of course, there must be different levels of "surprise" here—mild discombobulation versus dissociative, cognitive shock, for example. In a follow-up article, Ronald and Sipper (2001: 23) expand their argument to account for the observer's different "surprise states" with respect to systems engineering, where flabbergasting surprise—by definition—would be unwelcome.

> The more you think of "engineering with emergence," or *emergent engineering,* as we call it, the more it comes to resound oxymoronically. Emergent engineering, while inherently containing a non-evanescent element of surprise, seeks to restrict itself to what we call *unsurprising surprise:* though there is a persistent *L1–L2* understanding gap, and thus the element of surprise does not fade into oblivion, we wish, as it were, to take this surprise into our stride. Yes, the evolved robot works (surprise), but it is in some oxymoronic sense *expected* surprise: as though you were planning your own surprise birthday party.

Novelty may not be an entirely welcome phenomena in systems engineering, where predictability would seem to be at the heart of computation. Certainly this would account for critiques of Rodney Brooks's "out of control," reactive architectures in the 1990s. As Michael Woolridge (2002: 71) suggests: "One major selling point of purely reactive systems is that overall behaviour *emerges* from the interaction of the component behaviours when the agent is placed in its environment. But the very term 'emerges' suggests that the individual relationship between individual behaviours, environment, and overall behaviour is not understandable. This necessarily makes it hard to 'engineer' agents to fulfill specific tasks." It is therefore not surprising that strictly "reactive" architectures for robot agents are less common than hybrid approaches or approaches that use reactive or "vertical" architectures in order to evolve more effective systems (Woolridge 2002: 98). The irony of such corporations as *iRobot* (with Rodney Brooks as one of the founders) is that they use Brooks's "out of control" architectures (in varying degrees of hybrid approaches) to produce the absolutely quotidian (for example, the "Roomba" robot vacuum) and the all-too-predictable (military hardware).

What Ronald and Sipper suggest, though, is that "unsurprising surprise" displays, on some level, bad faith. Engineers can't afford the "bang" of real surprise, so they hedge their bets, limiting the dissonance to the multiagent equivalent of a whimper. As Hayles (1999: 232) indicates, artificial life simulations are rarely about producing absolute novelty so much as, for example, subjecting their Turing machine–cellular automata to "appropriately nonlinear processes so that the complex phenomenal world appears on its own." However, this is not merely an instance of engineering expediency; there's a politics to emergence.

Much of the popularity of Artificial Life simulations in the 1980s and 1990s stemmed from their seeming confirmation of hegemonic US discourses on race, gender, identity, and free markets. Hagiographies of Artificial Life stress the "shock of recognition" of the observer as the status quo emerged autochthonously from their self-organizing systems, for example, in Jonathan Rauch's (2002: 36) portrait of AL ancestor Thomas Schelling:

> One day in the late 1960s, on a flight from Chicago to Boston, he found himself with nothing to read and began doodling with pencil and paper. He drew a straight line and then "populated" it with Xs and Os. Then he decreed that each X and O wanted at least two of its six nearest neighbors to be of its own kind, and he began moving them around in ways that would make more of them content with their neighborhood. ... In the first frame blues and reds are randomly distributed. But they do not stay that way for long, because each agent, each simulated person, is ethnocentric. That is, the agent is happy only if its four nearest neighbors (at each point of the compass) include at least a certain number of agents of its own color.

From these initial conditions, Schelling generates racial segregation, demonstrating that the shape of Chicago or Boston (to name two highly segregated US cities) "naturally" emerges from the desire to be near at least some of one's own kind. But is this so natural? There are lots of assumptions here, among them: (1) the anhistorical assumption of stable, racial phenotypes as the basis for residence and (2) an atomistic individualism that construes residence as a "free" choice. The effect of Schelling's simulation is, of course, to exonerate over one hundred years of systematic racial discrimination at every level of urban development in the United States, from restrictive covenants and redlining to unequal public education and "Not In My Backyard" policies that all but insure that prisons and incinerators will be built in economically disadvantaged, non-white neighborhoods. Is the "natural," self-organization of segregation really a surprise? Or is it, in the tradition of multiagent systems engineering, a case of "unsurprising surprise"? That is, having established that race is the determinant factor in residence, what can the possible outcomes of the Turing machine be? If a pattern emerges from the cellular automata, it would have to be a "racial" pattern. Other simulations (for example, SimCity) also hinge on the "shock of recognition," that is, the emergence of the recognizable (Collins 2006). This self-fulfilling emergence delivers the "new" under controlled conditions that ensure that novelty mirrors the world we think we know (Helmreich 1998).

Similarly, appropriations of the science of complexity into New Economy theories that preached management on the "edge of chaos" (Lewin 1999) eschewed what were construed to be ossified organizational structures for flexible, "matrix"-style structures and open offices. Employees were cautioned to expect constant change; "visionary" entrepreneurship attracted speculative investments: "Where managers once operated with a machine model of their world, which was predicated on linear thinking, control, and predictability, they now find themselves struggling with something more organic and nonlinear, where limited control and a restricted ability to predict are the norm" (Terranova 2004: 197). In a "chaotic" environment, the New Economy business climate was conceived in the same way as simulations of Artificial Life, that is, as a self-organizing system from which novel organization, ideas, and structures might emerge. In Lewin's terms, "It is possible in principle to think of any business ecosystem in terms of a network of companies, each occupying a place in its own landscape of possibilities, and each landscape being coupled to many others: those of competitors, collaborators, and complementors" (1999: 207). Indeed, the Sante Fe Institute was bankrolled by venture capital trying to prosper amid "chaos." But, despite their eventual fate following the 2000 "dot.com" bust, venture capitalists needn't have worried much: what "emerged" out of the New Economy was a paradigmatic example of "unsurprising surprise." Like Schelling's model of residential segregation, multiple assumptions made the "out of control" economy rather less of a shock; corporations and profit make up the basic "units" for this Turing machine, and we shouldn't be overly surprised when flexible labor, state-supported exploitation, and widespread ecological devastation "arise" from what only management gurus and their readership could really construe as self-organizing systems. As in linear evolutionism, there are only two ways to go in this "out of control" system—toward more profitability for shareholders or less. The end of the New Economy in an orgy of speculative failures and accounting scandals is less a challenge to fundamentals of capitalism than a confirmation of their hegemony. Fundamental—and devastating—instances of "surprising surprise" will have to wait, as it were, for the revolution.

What about anthropology? Heir to the postmodern condition, cultural anthropologists seized upon a succession of what were thought to be emergent, liberatory identities and relationships: resistance, transnationals, subalterns, and cyborgs. Each of these, initially proposed by people positioned at the foreground of the field, suggested a novel modality somehow transcendent of the conditions that enabled its emergence. For example, anthropologists like Arjun Appadurai and Ulf Hannerz initially heralded the "cosmopolitan" as altering "the basis of cultural reproduction," challenging anthropology and even ushering in a new cultural politics where "deterritorialization" may discomfit all sorts of stable identities (Appadurai 1996: 49). Subsequent critics, however, questioned the extent to which "cosmopolitanism" might be described as a "new" phenomenon at all, and identified historical and present configurations as elite, Western-centered phenomena placing culture and citizenship in the service of capital (Brennan 2002; Ong 2002; Tsing 2000). Indeed, what Craig Calhoun terms a "soft cosmopolitanism" grounded in "frequent flyer lounges" and luxury hotels together with the globe-trotting perambulations of China's "parachute families" or Korea's "kirolki kajok" would certainly seem to confirm that cosmopolitanism is simply the superheated corona to neo-liberal regimes (2002: 873). Salman Rushdie, Pico Iyer, and a host of World Bank officers aside, the nation-state seems more powerful than ever—or at least certain nations-states. But how different is that from previous eras of imperialism? It's telling that contemporary evocations of the cosmopolitan look less to its novelty and transcendence than to the Enlightenment and to progressive movements in the early twentieth century (Mignolo 2000). If there's a politics to be derived from the cosmopolitan, it will not come from a break with the past, but from its continuity.

In anthropology, as elsewhere, the "emergent" future appears, not as genuine difference, but as lugubrious variations on a theme, recapitulations of the "discounted future" that makes up the endless horizon of an advanced capitalism that seems both present and proleptic. "Cyborg" worlds of fecund hybridity can, after all, be folded back into regimes of hyper-capital and commodified simulacra. As Strathern (1992: 61) warns, "Instead of the potential of unexpected combinations, unique individuals and unplanned effects, the future seems increasingly trapped by present choice." Proleptic futures emerging in the present easily become the endless present, a hall of mirrors where we misrecognize endless iterations of the "Now" as emerging change. Potentially revolutionary "machine assemblages" are said to emerge, but the initial surprise fades into languorous repetition, as the novel is quickly subtended into a continuously expanding universe of lively commodities. Like a joke to which you already know the ending, the end product is (literally) a product: unsurprising surprise. But could it have been different?

The late 1990s and early millennium gave many theorists on the left new hope that critical, cultural alterity could "emerge." But what is most striking about the above examples is the obdurate absence of emergence. This is one of the dangers attendant in the notion self-organizing systems: mythologies of autochthony obscure the structural over determination of putatively "emergent" results. In other words, there is an obstinate refusal to reflexively include the observer in the system. We can, it seems obvious now, regard the "New Economy" as "new" only from a certain perspective—an uninformed shareholder or hapless 401k investor, for example. Were we to examine the system from the position of a minimum-wage employee, would the "New Economy" look quite so "emergent"? Looking back over the changes in cybernetics since the advent of the field in the Macy Conferences of the 1940s, Hayles (1999: 447) notes: "Like homeostasis, reflexivity does not altogether disappear but lingers on as an allusion that authenticates new elements. It performs a more complex role than mere nostalgia, however, for it also leaves its imprint on the new constellation in the possibility that the virtual space can close on itself to create an autopoietic world sufficient unto itself, independent of the larger reality in which it is embedded." That is to say, in the area of artificial life, autonomous agents, and emergent behaviors, the observer no longer perturbs the system; instead, the system closes about the observer, reducing the kinds of dynamic perspectivism implicit in Varela's "enaction" to a single, hypostatized perspective: reflexivity as tableau vivant. This is what ontologically grounds the "lie" of Artificial Life: the universalization of a single perspective, like a first-person shooter game, limits the perspectives one can take, and therefore impoverishes alternatives.

Walter Benjamin's Arcades Project—among other things—looks to social and cultural production organized under the commodity. It is the commodity that produces the "eversame" under the guise of the new. For Benjamin, more than the exploitative relations it supports, the most trenchant critique of commodified social life is its torturous dullness (Jennings 2003). We live, as Benjamin says, in a world where "the soulless luxuriance of the furnishings becomes true comfort only in the presence of a dead body" (1978: 65). The "aura" causes us to misrecognize the deadly sameness of these seemingly mercurial and protean (but always repetitive) fashions as something genuinely new. By the end of the nineteenth century, these commodity chains explode into stentorian expositions of state progress, into the "phantasmagoria" that subtends even the most critical gaze into what Buck-Morrs (1989: 92) calls the "semantics of progress." "Bigger" and "more" are the source of fin-de-siecle enchantment, but the effect of this unsurprising surprise is to close down alternatives rather than open up the new. In fact, as Benjamin, Herbert Marcuse, and many others have shown, the point is to neutralize all opposition to capitalism by subsuming even the most revolutionary configurations under the sigil of the commodity.

In the New Economy, the same Lethean maneuver conjures emergence only by bracketing the observer, that is, it's "new" only if we ignore the Victorian Age–style exploitation of workers abroad and in sweat-shops in the US—only "emergent," that is, from the perspectives of people who misrecognize corporations as agents acting freely without the support of national governments, armies, and paramilitary forces. The cosmopolitan appears emergent only if we pretend that capital isn't mobile across putatively national boundaries, only if we sublimate the historic perambulations of global elites, only if we pretend that "nationality" is an undifferentiated identity uninflected by class, race, and ethnicity.

QUELLE BONNE SURPRISE!

But what would "surprising surprise" look like? Well, it would involve double surprise, as it were: initial surprise resulting in a hermeneutic singularity, surprise to the second power. This would involve successive disruptions in the formation of a multiagent system made up of observer, observed, and dynamic environment: (1) being surprised at the perceived behavior, and (2) appreciating of the perspective of the observer that ontologically grounds the surprise, thereby (3) causing the observer to take on a different, albeit triangulated, perspective on the system of which she is part and, (4) being surprised again at the resulting system formed with the new position of the observer.

Our own research has tried to evoke emergence through the formation of multiagent systems consisting of human agents interacting with nonhuman agents, that is, software agents and robots (Collins and Trajkovski 2006). For example, in one of our projects on human-robot interactions, we present groups of four to five volunteers with a problem: they must guide or coax a robot from a starting place on one side of a table to a finish line on the other. The robot is outfitted with different sensor-actuators combinations—sonar, light, and sound—and the goal of the exercise is to discover how to interact with the robot effectively. Volunteers use their own bodies, voices, and clothing to stimulate movement and obstacle avoidance in the robot agents who, accordingly, are either attracted to or repulsed from the human actions. Reviewing the video tapes of these sessions, we were struck by the synchronized, machinic grace formed by the sum of humans and robot as they slowly coordinated their movements. Is there emergence here? If so, it lies neither with the human agents guiding the robot (for which the robot's programming, once understood, allows the human agents to unproblematically stimulate the robot-agent's movements), nor with the robot itself (to which the human agents exist only as obstacles). Nor, I would argue, is there true emergence in the synchronized movements of human and robot agents. Instead, we would have to go back and use this experiment on humans and robots to reflect on the process by which we, a human and machinic entity composed of observer and observing machines, are also engaged in the same disciplining practice, perhaps to see human-robot and observer-camera-human-robot as networked translations of agency, each actant in the chain occupying an uneasy space (after Bruno Latour and Michel Serres) as a quasi-object.

Whether or not this constitutes "surprising surprise" is another question; we will only know the truly new when we see it, and even then we shouldn't hastily attach the label to social and cultural life. Utilizing "surprising surprise" in anthropological research doesn't mean keeping a scorecard of cognitive/cultural dissonance, but extends the hope that a radically different society lies within the (eventual) purview of the anthropological imaginary; as Stephen Tylor (1986) has said of ethnography in general, the "evocation" of alterity rather than its delineation. What Fredric Jameson (2005:46) writes of utopic thinking applies as well to emergence: "Its function lies not in helping us to imagine a better future but rather in demonstrating our utter incapacity to imagine such a future—our imprisonment in a non-utopian present without historicity or futurity—so as to reveal the ideological closure of the system in which we are somehow trapped and confined."

Emergence should not only gesture to the new, but also utterly restructure the old; not just the revelation of new sites of hybridity, but a devastating interrogation of the supervenient states from which emergence issued. Shock, trauma, visceral pain; these are the sorts of affective responses to a "surprising surprise" that threatens the ideological closure with the radically new, like positive feedback that renders homeostasis impossible and quickly overloads the system. In my favorite Zen koan, Dol Um is a Zen master attempting to "wake" the mind of a child:

> Dol Um led him to a rice paper window and poked a tiny hole. "You must sit here and look through this hole until a great big cow comes into the hole. Only watch for this big cow. When it comes, you will understand your true self."
>
> So the child only ate, slept, and looked through the hole in the rice paper. "When will the cow come?" His very clear child's mind held only this one question. One day passed, two days, almost one hundred days, when one day the hole grew bigger and bigger, and a huge cow appeared—"*Mooooo!*" "Waaaaaah-hhh!" the boy cried out. "Master! Master! The cow has come!" Dol Um rushed over and slapped his face. "Where is the cow now?" (Sahn 1997: 197)

NOTES

This chapter has been previously published as "Anthropology, Emergence and the Shock of the Foregone," *After Culture* 1(1) (2007). The author would like to thank the publication for permission to use the material here.

1. For a discussion of the place of computers in utopian (comp-utopian) or dystopian (compu-tropian) schemes, see Hakken and Andrews (1993).
2. This, of course, (mis)quoted from Marx's *18ᵗʰ Brumaire of Louis Napoleon.*
3. Science and Technology Studies (STS) marks both a departure and a subterranean return to this theme. On the one hand, anthropologies of science and technology give up authority over their objects of study (it is no longer possible to authoritatively opine about "my" science). On the other hand, STS lays claim to a certain form of prescience: authority lies in the privileged insight these anthropologists have on future cultures.
4. This kind of research constitutes a kind of futures investment on the part of anthropologists: i.e., examining the ramifications of emerging discourses on filiation may pay handsome dividends in the future. It is a reminder that anthropologists are not separable from the social and cultural contexts in which they work.

Conclusion

The Open Future

William Gibson, whose otherwise Gernsbackian evocations of cyberspace in *Neuromancer* have been cited for their prescience, can also be credited with shifting the topography of the future away from Heinlein's Wild West to Japan and East Asia. In *Idoru, Pattern Recognition*, and other books and short stories, Japan appears as both mise-en-scène and as catalyst for cultural change: the world, in other words, becomes more "Japanese," i.e., a highly stereotypical Japan associated in the United States with cell phones and anime. As he said in an interview in 1989,

> And I think that at one time the world believed that America was the future, but now the future's gone somewhere else, perhaps to Japan, it's probably on its way to Singapore soon but I don't think we're "it" anymore. (Gibson 1989)

Of course, in many ways, there's no "future" anymore either; or, rather, the gap between future and present has narrowed to what Veronica Hollinger (2006) calls the "future-present." As the ways in which media represent the contemporary present have grown to resemble Gibson's stylistic noir-thrillers, so the future itself has contracted into the present: the future is not "future Tokyo"; the future *is* Tokyo.

> Dining late, in a plastic-draped gypsy noodle stall in Shinjuku, the classic cliché better-than-*Bladerunner* Tokyo street set, I scope my neighbor's phone as he checks his text messages. Wafer-thin, kandy kolor pearlescent white, complexly curvilinear, totally ephemeral looking, its screen seethes with a miniature version of Shinjuku's neon light show. He's got the rosary-like anticancer charm attached; most people here do, believing it deflects microwaves, grounding them away from the brain. It looks great, in terms of a novelist's need for props, but it may not be the next generation in terms of what I'm used to back here. (Gibson 2001)

Gibson's is a temporally chiasmatic Tokyo—it is the future, the present, and, as we read this two decades later, also the past of the future. In his writings, gadgetry is more advanced, corporations more menacing, virtual lives more textured, but there's little difference between Gibson's fiction and the slightly creepy *Wired* magazine column that ran in the 1990s, "Japanese Schoolgirl Watch," where journalists play peeping tom for the sake of upcoming techno-fashion. There's no need for a time machine. Here, Gibson *qua* anthropologist can see both present and future interpenetrating in sexually charged evocations of telematic product.

But in a sense, there is something recidivistically nineteenth century about all of this. Rather than travel to the past by visiting the cultural other, here we travel to the future. But both places are (spatially) oriented on the same timeline. Indeed, Gibson is merely recharging the old orientalist machine, still running on the same dichotomies of West and its others, still banking on the same racist machine (Sohn 2008). If we wanted to know about "stone age" life, we could visit aboriginal groups (our past). Likewise, if we want to know about products and trends, we need only visit Shinjuku and watch for schoolgirls fumbling with their *keitai* or go to an anime convention to see what the *manga otaku* are up to. Gibson's time machine may run counter to the nineteenth-century imagination, but it's still the old time machine, and one need only read the newspaper to see the ease with which J. G. Frazer's temporalizations are charged up and ready to go. And this time machine, whether in the nineteenth century or the twenty-first, starts and ends with the West, with white people, with elites; the default setting, in other words, is modernity itself.

In contrast, I wrote this last chapter while on a Fulbright grant in Seoul, South Korea, a city filled with a surfeit of technological geegaws, to be sure (ubiquitous broadband, universal smartphone ownership, etc.), and yet, unlike Gibson, I don't see Korea as "the future," i.e., some prescient glimpse onto the next thing in information technology. There's too much here to upset such a linear vision: a strong labor movement, a continued legacy of colonial domination from the United States, the continued partitioning of the peninsula into North and South. But in this we might glimpse a sense of people trying to forge a Korean future at odds with the IMF-inflected futures forced upon Korea and other Asian nations in the late 1990s, that is, even in a country at the very core of advanced capitalism (South Korea is the world's eleventh largest economy), we still might be able to grasp—or evoke—alternatives to the present. Those alternatives, I hope, will lead to justice, to decolonization, and to reunification (on many levels). None of those futures can be easily appropriated into Western discourse—these are Korean futures we're talking about, not the future of modernity. To engage these futures is to acknowledge the colonialism that has underlain figurations of Western futures over the past 150 years. And it is here that anthropologists might best harness the critical power of culture.

This book has taken anthropology into places in which it is ordinarily not associated: SF, NASA, futurism, biogenetics. The purpose has been to show how anthropology has both contributed to speculations on cultural futures, on the one hand, and sketched ways that anthropology might contribute to reinvigorating the future as a site for radical alternatives, on the other. As I have suggested, this can happen in at least two ways: (1) anthropological futures can provide alternatives to Western-dominated discourse on progress and technology and (2) anthropological analyses of emergences might even intervene in the process of future imaginings. In this final chapter, I draw some of those strands together to suggest how anthropological work may contribute to a resurgence of the critical power of the future itself, what we might call the utopian, not, as it is ordinarily understood, as transcendental and idealistic but, after the work of Fredric Jameson, as a means of approaching the limits of critical thought in the age of globalization and thereby gesturing to future difference that, by definition, cannot yet be articulated. Such an anthropology may work to finally dismantle the time machine, understood here as the suspect manipulation of chronotypes for the production of knowledge. In doing so, anthropology may help to "free" time, i.e., to realize its creative, critical power in what Henri Bergson terms "duration."

LOOKING FOR ANTHROPOLOGICAL ANCESTORS

It is easy to see Mead's clumsy, wartime attempts at engineering culture as an ultimately egregious direction for anthropology to take: di Leonardo's critique of Mead's hubris attributes her penchant for social engineering to her parents, who taught at the Wharton School, authored early tracts on advertising and, in many ways, anticipated the "cultural turn" in corporations in the 1990s wherein "culture" is discovered as a fungible, "value-added" commodity.

There are a multitude of reasons for anthropology's eventual turn away from this kind of cultural tinkering, the least of which, of course, is that is doesn't even work. After all, with culture's famous polysemy, who could even agree on what exactly culture *is* long enough to sculpt the contour of its future? The idea that one could develop cultures out of whole cloth belongs to a 1950s science fiction novel. Or does it?

The irony is that di Leonardo's critique of Mead is accurate on at least two levels: New Economy business strategies in the 1990s demonstrate a close kinship with Mead's concept of the engineered future by attempting to engineer the very cultures she dreamed up at her Orwellian worst. For example, in Andrew Ross's ethnography of dot-com start-ups, *No Collar: the Humane Workplace and Its Hidden Costs* (2003), executives at Razorfish attempt to engineer a "culture" of creativity in order to maximize emergence. As Ross (2003) recounts,

> In the firm's heyday, all new recruits were issued a book titled, "Razorfish Creative Mission." . . . "Creativity" in all its forms was the core value, and it was celebrated on every page, though mostly in an unchewed lingo that aped Business English: "We are working toward an improved efficiency where new kinds of thinking expand the limits of intelligent thought. Unprecedented thinking often comes into being in a nonlinear manner. Opposites, inconsistencies, and ambiguities produce creative sparks."

Inspired by the kinds of complexity generated in Artificial Life demonstrations, Razorfish explicitly tried to encourage the eccentric by hiring the idiosyncratic and allowing them to follow their own, individual orbits. In doing so, they hoped to remain on the "edge of chaos," i.e., be able to adapt to rapid changes in the economy and prosper amid postmodern, creative destruction. During the 1990s, their bold strategies paid off, and Razorfish expanded offices across the United States and into Europe.

By the time of the "crash" in 2000, however, the lavish parties and aggressive iconoclasm seemed more like posturing than a business strategy, and Razorfish, after downsizing its workforce, crafted a more conservative image for its clients. The executives who stayed at Razorfish accordingly rolled with the changes and offered Ross their more sober assessments of "creative culture" at the US corporation:

> In the period of time I had been interviewing Habacker, she seemed to have accepted that "Value" always had a flip side in the business world. Many of the qualities that she and her cohort had once cherished had become liabilities as the company's direction shifted. Now she was learning that the profile she had favored in recruiting others at Razorfish–eccentric, self-motivated and self-disciplined individuals–was just as likely to be a handicap elsewhere.

That is, the emergence of the new had been one business strategy among others and, in a different climate, one could simply change the company's homepage, hire people with predilections for conservative suits, and move on. That is, whatever "culture" one might engineer for the future, one thing would never change: the market itself. As Ross (2003: 210) suggests,

> Despite these criticisms, there was a more general acceptance among fish that no one really had control over the company's financial destiny. The market was

perceived as an unchallenged authority that was somehow denying the company permission to succeed, and very little could be done about it.

That is, "culture" might be engineered, but it is, for all intents and purposes, window dressing to a political economy assumed as both the natural state of things and the teleological end of history. "Emergence" is just a small blip in the geometric progression toward a perfect market, not the future but a localized, temporal eddy in the grand narrative of a liberal capitalism that marks the end of history. That is, just as the elemental units of the system are literally "naturalized" (as an ecosystem), the ultimate teleology is never in doubt.

In a way, this was the fullest realization of culture engineering. It meant encouraging creative "play"—structuring workplaces to deny hierarchy in a way eerily similar to Mead's prescriptions for "emergent clusters." But, subordinate to the market, it was a lie—there was still hierarchy, as employees learned after the dot-com crash, and "play" was, moreover, not really playful at all. In the dust of the dot-com bust, the paeans to culture in the business world have become less frequent; it is hard, after all, to differentiate them from simple propaganda, an issue that Mead, Bateson, and Benedict, among others, also faced in their meditations on engineering culture.

Part of the critique of cultural anthropology in the 1960s was precisely over this effort at engineering, particularly as it pertained to development work and modernization. Of course, the efforts of the state to engineer a modernist future have since been supplanted by private NGOs, whose programs to spur neoliberal "development" must be seen as the return of a curious time paradox, for while 1960s development was resolute in its linearity, NGO development hinges on the restoration of nature, an eternal return to a social Darwinist capitalism (cf. Escobar 1995, 2001; Ferguson 2002). That is, the IMF and the World Bank, together with NGOs in their service, proffer a future that is at once ineluctable for a country that accedes to US-style industrialization (à la W. W. Rostow's stages) while being, at the same time, a return to nature where life may be "nasty, brutish, and short" for most but not, at least, for the stockholders.

Having given up on cultural engineering, the sorts of cultural futures of a properly postmodern anthropology have been more modest. Claiming, on the one hand, that true representations of the cultural other are impossible, while at the same time vouchsafing the authority of anthropology to still tender its (partial) truths, "engineering" a future in contemporary anthropology may be altogether impossible, although recusing itself on the basis of the incommensurability of cultural others connotes a kind of future—which is the continuation of the past. In *Anthropology as Cultural Critique* (now thirty years old), Marcus and Fischer (1986: 1) draw on the Boasian heritage (via Herder) to suggest the role of anthropology as cultural relativism gadfly:

> The other promise of anthropology, one less fully distinguished and attended to than the first, has been to serve as a form of cultural critique for ourselves. In using portraits of other cultural patterns to reflect self-critically on our ways, anthropology disrupts common sense and makes us reexamine our taken-for-granted assumptions.

This is hardly a novel insight into anthropology—Oliver was making the same point in the 1960s, and the Boasians before him in the 1920s. What's unclear from this is the direction—cultural critique toward what? Having disrupted the commonsense assumptions of progress, the future, power, and individualism, do you then forge a better society? A more tolerant one? At its worst, the kind of "cultural critique" promoted by Marcus et al. could be construed as cultural essentialism through the back door, where the re-alization of the Other leads, if not to the naturalization of common sense, then to the hypostatization of cultures themselves, each spinning in its own time space. Culture may disrupt our common sense, but its function is not to undermine the West or point the way toward an alternative future. In a way, it seals off culture at the same time as accessing it; the recognition of difference in the other is simultaneously the legitimation of the status quo in the self. Inexorably, perhaps, this has led to the exhaustion of this vein, despite Marcus's injunction for a multisited anthropology that purports to more ably follow lines of power while, perhaps, simply remaining within the ambit of globalization and power and relegating local understandings to NGOs (cf. Hendry 1999).

Indeed, as Samuel Gompers said of the trade unions, "We do want more": many anthropologists have been asking for more from their field. From Wolf on through Faye Harrison (and beyond), a whole lineage of anthropologists dissatisfied with the theoretical navel-gazing of an anthropology stuck on issues of representation has struggled toward a politically engaged anthropology. Much of this critique is sited in the Americas—especially Caribbean and Latin American countries. Reviving a more activist anthropology suppressed by McCarthyism (cf. Price 2004) means returning to the image of an anthropology that can change the world: it is telling that cultural relativism in the strictly anthropological sense (understanding cultures as integrated wholes both rational and intelligible to members within that culture) was not considered threatening to Hoover's FBI; the idea, however, that anthropology could contribute to a better world defined by less pernicious inequalities, etc., was considered a challenge to the *Pax Americana.*

Hale (2006: 97) describes the chief difference between this approach and the
more retiring "cultural critique" aesthetic:

> By *activist research*, I mean a method through which we affirm a political align-
> ment with an organized group of people in struggle and allow dialogue with
> them to shape each phase of the process, from conception of the research topic
> to data collection to verification and dissemination of the results.

The future envisioned by the people studied and the anthropologist's vision
of that same trajectory intersect at the anthropological record produced. But
while what Hale is calling an "activist anthropology" has its precursors in
the work of Sol Tax and others, there's a distinct sense of leaving the "utopian" longings of cultural engineers for something more realpolitik; acting
in the capacity of the activist means, by definition, that anthropologists leave
the "no-place" of theoretical conjecture for something by definition compro-
mised by lines of power.

But although this work is vital to the continuing relevance of anthropology, there is still something missing; isn't working within development and
international politics affirming those discourses (however negatively)? As
Besteman and Gusterson (2005: 2) complain of the work of media pundits
in the introduction to their edited collection,

> Although they do not come from the same side of the political map, they draw
> on and embellish a loosely coherent set of myths about humans and culture
> that have a strange staying power in American public discourse: that conflicts
> between people of different cultures, races, or genders is inevitable; that biology
> is destiny; that cultures are immutable; that terrible poverty, inequality, and
> suffering are natural; and that people in other societies who do not want to live
> just like Americans are afraid of "modernity."

It is the conscientious anthropologist who advocates for the people they've
worked with, even more so the anthropologist who intervenes in the ubiquitous, nested power relations in a world of globalization. However, Besteman and Gusterson seem to be suggesting, à la Lakoff (2004) and others
(Chomsky, for example), that the tropological space underlying the production of pundit discourse itself needs to be challenged, the dull recitations of
"pros" and "cons," deracinating social and political complexities to the safe
torpor of stereotypical binarisms of West and rest.

But it is not just enough to puncture these ballooning mythic cycles
of universalism with cultural particulars—anthropologists have been doing
this, even in the bad, old nineteenth century (and before). The goal should
be to allow these cultural footnotes to the grand myths of the West to cas-

cade into an ultimately destructive arc of emergent differentiations where "other" futures undermine "our" futures and, in the shifting terrain, suggest the possibility of difference. This does not mean some Don Juan–esque conjuration of the cultural other as our ticket to authenticity but, in many ways, its opposite: the evocation of the unthinkable, at least from the perspective of present hegemony. What is needed, according to Jameson, is a resurgence of the utopian; the conjuration of the impossible through the evocation of the limits of discourse.

If we look beyond Mead qua cultural engineer (as indeed we should), there are other anthropological ancestors that might be invoked. I began this book with a look back at nineteenth-century anthropology's time machine: the ways it has slotted (and continues to slot) people along a continuum of development and temporality. In many ways, the "slipstream" of anthropology continues on, with even putatively sympathetic portrayals of people imprisoning culture in the past even as these ethnographies purport to engage them coevally.

Here, Alfred Russel Wallace is a case in point. While his travels to Malaysia may have made him more sympathetic to non-Western peoples, and his own Owenite leanings more committed to human equality, he nevertheless shared with his contemporaries a bedrock racism that continually invoked "savages" who didn't need their innate mental capacities for their everyday life (Kottler 1974). This was one of his arguments against natural selection as an explanatory frame for humans. "Savages" didn't "need" their vast mental capacity, hence their development could only be due to some "higher" agency. Moreover, his dreams of an eventual human equality—the same ones that enraged his 1864 contemporaries at the Anthropological Society of London—were nevertheless based on the extinction of "savage" peoples.

But Wallace is still worth thinking about, if only for his thoughts on the future. Some comparison is probably in order. Like Wallace, Darwin, in his 1871 *The Descent of Man*, looks to some future point when "the civilised races of man will almost certainly exterminate and replace throughout the world the savage races" (Darwin 1871: 1:201). The tradeoff here is that "civilized" morality will likewise prove ascendant: "In this case the struggle between our higher and lower impulses will be less severe, and virtue will be triumphant" (Darwin 1871: 1:104). Of course, this would be little consolation to people exterminated by the "civilized." Like Wallace, Darwin reiterates the racism and imperialism of his day: his prognostications are very much part of his evolutionary theory, and it is here that Darwin seems very close indeed to the racist, cultural evolutionism of Herbert Spencer.

But this is where Wallace and Darwin split. After his famed 1864 paper corroborating Darwin's theories, Wallace—shortly after his first experience of a séance—became a ready convert to spiritualism. Convinced of nonmaterial intelligences, he carved out an exception to the natural selection he found among the world's flora and fauna. "By 1869, in an article that he contributed to the *Quarterly Review*, Wallace was ready to suggest that natural selection could neither explain the emergence of human intelligence nor account for man's distinguishing moral qualities. These, he indicated, might better be explicated by the directive actions of a guiding mind" (Oppenheim 1985: 314–15)). This "new branch of Anthropology" meant acknowledging nonhuman and nonmaterial intellectual and moral agents, spiritual beings who, Wallace increasingly came to believe, were guiding the course of humanity into a utopian future characterized by radical equality. "Wallace embraced spiritualism with all his heart, because it perfectly suited his deepest desire to design a new world view for himself—one where the influence of Robert Owen, Henry George, and Edward Bellamy figured prominently, and where the theory of natural selection underwent substantial modification" (Oppenheim 1985: 302).

The "split"—and it really was a split—seems to have baffled many historians, who found it difficult to believe Wallace's incredible credulity toward what scientists like Huxley and Darwin viewed as the mountebank's slight-of-hand. Oppenheim (1983), for example, can't get over the glaring contradiction of a scholar that insists on strict materialism for every other animal *except* humans, and for reasons that seem to have nothing to do with science at all.

But it would be mistake to reduce the Darwin/Wallace rupture to one of materialism versus Spiritualism. Darwin, as Desmond and More (1991) point out, theorized in the context of the industrial revolution, and it is no surprise that evolution (particularly in an emphasis on competition and fitness) fits the capitalism of the age. Under Darwin's scheme, animals performed as rational economic actors "to maximize some sort of self-interest—whatever their theory of animal psychology, or motivation, might be" (Graeber 2014). Moreover, for Darwin, it was the spirit of that capitalism that drove human futures. The triumph of "virtue" that would represent the triumph of the civilized was simultaneously the "triumph" of capitalism. Yet Wallace was critical of capitalism and saw its intractable inequalities becoming more and more pronounced in the final years of the nineteenth century. Nineteenth-century monopoly capitalism was hardly progress, and could only be remedied with land reform and socialism.

Much has been written about Spiritualism and progressivism. Many of the most fervent proponents of Spiritualism were also the progressives of their day: abolitionism, suffrage, pacifism. That these might all go together seems self-contradictory, yet they make perfect sense together from the perspective of activists who were marginalized from powerful and self-serving ranks of intellectuals and scientists (Braudge 1989). People like Victoria Woodhull (who ran for president of the United States with Frederick Douglass as her running mate) brought together all of these elements—feminism, spiritualism, anticapitalism, sexual freedom. Spiritualism not only elevated women to positions of power, it also gestured to an authority apart from the entrenched social order. It really was a window onto another world.

But there was another reason for the turn to Spiritualism. Darwin's theory was, on some level, a developmental narrative about the past, one that included numerous adaptations, sexual selections, and the rise and fall of populations. For Wallace, on the other hand, human intelligence and spirituality exceeded the present, indicating untold (and, perhaps, unknowable) potentials for a future human. It's this moment in Wallace's career that I wish to recover: this sense that there is a potential and a possibility that is not explicable from Wallace's present, one that, for him, is only visible in the partial shadows of the séance, the spirit photography, or slate writing. For others, this was a link to people who had passed on, but for Wallace—and for some of those who practiced Spiritualism as a formal religion—it was a clue to a utopian future. In other words, the future cannot be divined from discourses on modernity—at least not capitalist modernity.

A second moment. While Zora Neale Hurston has enjoyed greater and greater literary recognition over the past decades, her own anthropology is generally eclipsed by that of other, Boasian anthropologists: Margaret Mead, Ruth Benedict, Edward Sapir, Alfred Kroeber. Part of this is due to her racism-inflected marginalization from the field. But part is also due to her revolutionary anthropology, one that spanned textual genres and that suggests another direction for ethnographic work. Mixing anthropology, folklore, and fiction, Hurston's work differed from both her anthropological and her literary contemporaries, and she faced considerable backlash from all sides. Her reappraisal over the last decades, though, has renewed focus on her anthropology, one that concentrates on the future in a way that her contemporary Boasians never did. That said, a "future orientation" is not something generally appended to Hurston's work, and in anthropology she is chiefly remembered for her research in the US South, in Haiti, and in Jamaica on music, religion, and folklore.

Yet, Isiah Lavender III has suggested that *Their Eyes Were Watching God* (1937) is Afrofuturist in its emphasis on opening up the potential for other worlds: "A future horizon exists in this novel that has not been explored, where literalized metaphors, characteristic of sf, help explain a problematic black social experience. African Americans, who seemingly have no future, turn to folklore to create one, defying the protocols of a raced reality" (Lavender 2016: 215). It's important here to differentiate that from other early twentieth-century studies of "folklore" and "tradition." Alan Lomax's work documenting southern music (which Hurston also worked on) was very much premised on salvage—on the disappearance of folkways under the on- slaught of mass culture. Indeed, this was the impetus for his work as director of the Archives of American Folk Song (now the Archive of Folk Culture in the American Folklife Center) at the Library of Congress. And while Lomax certainly supported folklife as a living tradition, traditions didn't have a revolutionary, transformative potential. Hurston's approach, on the other hand, took folkways as a starting point for utopian processes. In her search for the possibility of an African American life free from the oppres- sions of life in "Eatonville," Hurston evokes the world-making potentials of speech, song, and narratives—"technologies" belonging to an Afrofuturist tradition that places her on par with other, early Afrofuturist writers like Du Bois and Schuyler. In Lavender's analysis, Hurston's protagonist Janie becomes "a creator of Southern black historical consciousness insofar as she resists the limitations of various oppressions by recovering a projec- tive trajectory," and *Their Eyes Were Watching God* an Afrofuturist text that "provides an image of tomorrow" (Lavender 2016: 229). More than Afrofu- turism, though, I would submit that Hurston's work (and, in a much more qualified way, Wallace's) orients us toward anthropologies that exceed themselves and help to articulate the critical worldmaking of the people with whom anthropologists study.

It is easy to dismiss the anthropologies described in this book as some- how ancillary to either anthropology as the description of cultures or an activist anthropology advocating culture change toward social justice. But I would submit that anthropology needs to take even larger imaginative leaps: the kinds of futures these anthropologists proffer differ (or can dif- fer) significantly from those of think tanks, congressional subcommittees, and television commercials, all of which endlessly recycle recapitulations of the same. It is necessary—and even vital—for anthropologists to engage the world in which they live through their areas of expertise. However, there is more to it than that. Anthropology needs to be part of the eventual project of transforming the discourses of modernity and modernization themselves, of creating spaces for alternatives to both present power inequalities and the institutions that support them as well as the discourses that naturalize them as the inevitable struggle between the "wealth of nations." That is to say, we have to see anthropology as part of a utopian project, although not the utopia we ordinarily think about.

Utopia is at the crux of the time machine anthropologists invented and H. G. Wells dramatized; it seems at once spatial (More's paradigmatic uto-

pia was, after all, a colonized island) as well as outside of space (literally
no-place), temporal (at the end of a line of progress) as well as standing out
of time (at the end of history). Peripheral to most academic discussions of
politics and culture, utopia is the object of a curious sublimation that, in
an appropriately Freudian way, finds its outlet in dreamlike worlds of contradictory images and neonatal philosophies. In what I regard as a fairly
illustrative example, Edward Rothstein (2003: 23) writes that

> it may be that the best we can hope for when it comes to utopias is that they be
> held at arm's length and regarded as aesthetic constructions, in which various
> proportions are neatly worked out, contradictions eliminated, and outside in-
> trusions minimized.

Of course, the possibility that utopia might actually be realized constitutes a
kind of "fear" (Jameson 2005: 154). Yet Rothstein, like many commentators
on the utopian, is unwilling to foreswear the utopian altogether:

> At any rate, however out of reach, most utopias are meant to be pursued. Uto-
> pias represent an ideal toward which the mundane world must reach. They
> are examples to be worked for. Utopianism creates a political program, giving
> direction and meaning to the idea of progress; progress is always on the way
> toward some notion of utopia. (Rothstein 2003: 3)

Rothstein is likewise ambivalent on the issue of utopia's time, pointing out
that "Utopia stands outside of history. It is the city on the hill, the society's
dream image" (2003: 8). But at the same time, utopia for Rothstein can define exactly what we mean by history:

> Much technological innovation, in fact, is driven by a kind of utopianism: some-
> thing new is introduced into the world that promises transformation. Technol-
> ogy is disruptive, sometimes destructive, displacing older procedures, products,
> and ideas. (Rothstein 2003: 16)

From the "citty upon a hill" to Silicon Valley, utopia underlies both the hope
for earthly salvation *and* the succession of new technologies, i.e., somehow
both outside of time and at heart of the very way in which we have understood time (as progress).

To simply dismiss Rothstein's essay as incongruous and self-contradictory
is to miss the point: in the utopian we can see the limits of the time machine;
dismantling it means more, after all, than just taking the keys away and
hoping for the best (as Wells's Time Traveller did), but subverting the concatenation of chronotypes that allows us to map these discrete timespaces

in the first place. As Jameson (2005: xiii) has commented, Utopia "can serve the negative purpose of making us more aware of our mental and ideological imprisonment (something I have myself occasionally asserted); and that therefore the best Utopias are those that fail the most comprehensively." Evoking the utopian means outlining the limits of time and space as master discourses of economy, culture, and progress. And dismantling these elements means gesturing to an entirely different temporality altogether. In other words, in thinking about the future of culture, what we need is a different conception of "future" itself, conceived of not as the end of Western progress but as the fecund brachiation of cultural possibilities. This means utopia as a process, one bound up with a commitment to Deleuze and Guattari's "new earth" and a "people to come" (Bogue 2011: 87).

THE BERGSONIAN TURN

Henri Bergson's writings (*Creative Evolution*, etc.) challenge the hegemony of time as an etiolated residue of spatialities. That is, Bergson takes on the task of evoking time as a real dimension, as the generative motor of possibility; in the process, Bergson reforms the future as a site for real change. For Deleuze (1991), this ultimately makes "time" a more precise concept for philosophy; for anthropology, Bergson promises to emancipate time from its subordination to teleological evolution where what's past is always prologue. Futures writings (*Megatrends*, *Powershift*) by definition project an array of possibilities based on extrapolations from the present. As "realistic" as these projected scenarios may seem, for Bergson, they represent an artificially closed environment. As Ansell-Pearson (2002: 75) explains,

> Such systems can be calculated ahead of time since they are being posited as existing prior to their realization in the form of possibles (when a possible gets realized it simply gets existence added to it, its fundamental nature has not changed). The successive states of this kind of system can be conceived as moving at any speed, rather like the unrolling of a film: it does not matter at what speed the shots run, an "evolution" is not being depicted.

Thus, when we think about the future, we think of it as a succession of frames moving at variable speed, a future unrolling before us. In Wells's *Time Machine*, for example,

> the twinkling succession of darkness and light was excessively painful to the eye. Then, in the intermittent darkness, I saw the moon spinning swiftly through her quarters from new to full, and had a faint glimpse of the circling stars.

Presently, as I went on, still gaining velocity, the palpitation of night and day merged into one continuous greyness; the sky took on a wonderful deepness of blue, a splendid luminous color like that of early twilight; the jerking sun became a streak of fire, a brilliant arch, in space; the moon a fainter fluctuating band; and I could see nothing of the stars, save now and then a brighter circle flickering in the blue. (Wells 1895: 66)

The Time Traveller represents the passage of time as diurnal succession—the phases of the moon, the arc of the sun. These spatial changes mark the passage of time, and, as the Time Traveller "accelerates" (again, spatially), the heavenly bodies rise and set faster, like a film speeding up. For Bergson, this may be the way we humans understand time as a matter of necessity, but it is not really an understanding of time per se. This, as Ansell-Pearson (2002: 23) reminds us, is the problem dogging Zeno's paradox, the confusion of space and time. But this spatialization of time results in simple Netwonian linearization: things persist (or do not) from one "frame" to the next. Certain things immanent in the present come to pass; others do not. In popular representations of globalization, these frames succeed each other quickly, in areas thought to be ancillary to globalization, the frames move slowly. What are the consequences of this? Deleuze (1991: 187) explains,

> The possible passes into the real through limitation, the culling of other possibilities. But through this resemblance and limitation, the real comes to be seen as *given* rather than made, as an inevitable outcome, merely waiting for real existence.
>
> On such a model, the possible is both more than but also less than the real. It is more insofar as the real selects from a number of possibles, limiting their profusion; but it is less insofar as it is the real minus existence. Realization is a process in which creativity and production have no place.

This is the conception of the future as the winnowing of possibles, a narrowing that leads to an outcome that—by definition—was inevitable all along. The kinds of cultural "futures" generated in this closed system invariably confirm one of the "possibles"; in terms of globalization, "possibles" include predictions of market crashes, openings of new markets, each corner of the world falling to multinational capital, rising Gini coefficients, etc. That is, the scope of "possible" futures here is one measured by *degree*: either there is *more* or *less* of the sorts of vectors of globalization we describe—inequality, transnational capital, speed, Westernization, etc. Even the possibility of future parity can be described according to *degree*: wage gaps can close or widen. This is not a question of perceiving the reality of present-day inequalities but of seeing unemployment, hunger, homelessness, etc., as "natural'," i.e., to be combated with policies and public spending, to be sure, but also to be *accepted* as part of the capitalist terrain.

Against this ataraxic conception of time and change, Bergson (via his latter-day apologist, Gilles Deleuze) proposes *duration*, out of a critique of the tendency science has to confuse *difference in degree* with *difference in kind*. As Deleuze writes (1991:31):

> The division occurs between (1) duration, which "tends" for its part to take on or bear all the differences in kind (because it is endowed with the power of qualitatively varying with itself), and (2) space, which never presents anything but differences of degree (since it is quantitative homogeneity).

Most famously, Bergson illustrates the difference (in *Mind and Memory*) in a glass of dissolving sugar:

> Take a lump of sugar: It has spatial configurations. But if we approach it from that angle, all we will ever grasp are differences in degree between that sugar and any other thing. But it also has a duration, a rhythm of duration, a way of being in time that is at least partially revealed in the process of its dissolving, and that shows how this sugar differs in kind not only from other things, but first and foremost from itself. (Deleuze 1991: 31–32)

Thus, duration admits difference in the act of making a difference; not something explicable in terms of degree (where time can be reduced to an axial rectangle on a histogram) but in terms of differences in kind; the world in which we exist partakes of a multiplicity of durations.

> It signifies that my own duration, such as I live it in the impatience of wait-ing, for example, serves to reveal other durations that beat to other rhythms, that differ in kind from mine. Duration is always the location and the environ-ment of differences in kind; it is even their totality and multiplicity. (Deleuze 1991: 32)

These are not to be confused with the multiplicity of time bubbles com-mon to the Victorian time machine, where "natives" are imprisoned in a past, Europeans in (their) future. It is instead to admit that lives develop in the context of a time that cannot be reduced to a single, chronopolitical scale. That is to say, duration admits of what Bergson terms a "virtual mul-tiplicity," a sort of unity of difference that itself differentiates itself in the process of *actualization* (here is Deleuze's approach to Bergson). We might look to one other example: that of games, each of which demands that we open ourselves to other durations. From this comes much of the game's frisson: the addiction of the game is precisely that it opens our experience onto "game time." And this is not merely a question of a game making us "speed up" or "slow down"; the "world" of the game admits of other durations.

The effect of this is not to make time a *negative* force whereby the future is winnowed away through a series of possibles, one of which will be selected to be the real, but a positive force, doubly differentiating between, on the one hand, a virtual (but not transcendent) difference and its differentiation in the act of becoming actualized, in the act of interacting with, accommodating, resisting, overcoming other durations. This, as Grosz (2004: 189) suggests, invests time with a creative power:

> The movement from a virtual unity to an actual multiplicity requires that there is a certain leap, this time a leap of innovation or creativity, the surprise that the virtual leaves within the actual. If realization is the concretization of a preexistent plan, program, or blueprint, by contrast, actualization is the opening up of the virtual to what befalls it.

That is, actualization, far from exhausting the "possible," actually opens up more virtualities; the future, then, should be understood less as the dismal consequences of the present than as the excess production of fecund contingencies.

The consequences of this for the study of culture are developed in Bergson's *Creative Evolution* (1983 [1944]), Bergson's far-reaching redefinition of Darwinism according to this central, generative principle of difference; he is largely forgotten in the twentieth century precisely on charges of vitalism, i.e., that he is investing a generative power in time itself rather than construing it as a neutral table upon which spatial movements might be charted. But construing evolution as actualizations of a virtual makes evolution a creative act. Ansell-Pearson (2002: 75) defends Bergson from these charges:

> One of the difficulties we have in accepting this conception of duration as the invention of the new is due to the way we think of evolution as the domain of the realization of the possible. We have difficulty in thinking that an event— where a work of art or a work of nature—could have taken place unless it were not already capable of happening. For something to become it must have been possible all along (a conception of logical-spatial-possibility).

One of the lingering "survivals" of nineteenth-century social Darwinism is to see cultural developments as inevitable: this is the "general" evolution that, for example, places space colonization at the apex of a human evolution from the Acheulian hand axe on up. In more recent terms, the kinds of trajectories of globalization (Malthusian disaster, ecological ruin, rapid modernization) are construed as the inevitable realizations of an ineluctably evolving capitalist system. The idea of true *difference* is left behind.

Culture construed as virtuality, on the other hand, foregrounds culture as pure difference; actualizations of cultural difference not only fail to exhaust the potentials of a virtual multiplicity, but they also enrich the virtual (here coincident with the past) with potential as yet unactualized (but no less real). Grosz (2004: 186) explains:

> This is what life (or consciousness) brings to the world: the remembrance of the past, the history submerged or lying behind the present, whose resources are not completely depleted for they reinvigorate the present and help generate the new, which, for Bergson, is precisely the movement of actualization of the virtual. Duration is the subsistence of the past in the present and the capacity of this to generate an unexpected future beyond that of imminent action.

As life is actualized, virtualities do not drop away like possibilities unrealized but form the resources for new lines of actualization, novel, and productive difference inexplicable from the present lines of actualization.

This, for Grosz, signals the importance of history. But the study of cultural histories (and cultural presents) does the same thing. How do we envision the cultural future? Where do we look? The entire human experience becomes constitutive of culture's virtuality. Not only the entire human past but also the virtual multiplicities of human lifeways all double back to exist (in what Bergson calls a highly contracted form) in the present. To say that, pace the Boasians, the study of culture denaturalizes or relativizes is not enough, since it renaturalizes, as it were, the incommensurability of culture. Instead, the study of others discloses other durations, other actualizations that form the resources for other virtualities. Anthropology here is still descriptive, but it is also catalyzing, energizing, and morphogenetic. Can anthropology change the world by writing about the future?

Absolutely: the mistake in thinking otherwise is to consider the future already delimited by the present choices. People who consider themselves "realistic" may try to, say, soften the blow of American hegemony abroad (as do Rorty, Barber, and even, in his less virulent writings, Fukuyama) by arguing for a liberal cosmopolitanism, but the idea of a world without American hegemony or capitalism is seen as simply fanciful. And yet, consonant with Bergson, we can suggest that this world is *real*—virtualities waiting to be actualized. In describing leftist political movements, anarchist conventions, and union meetings, anthropologists are not *predicting* a future, nor are they necessarily even advocating that these organizations become a blueprint for other activist movements. What they are doing, though, is elucidating actualizations as virtualities for future actualization, which, accordingly, will in turn differentiate themselves from what came before. For Grosz (2004: 186), this is the function of history qua difference.

Cultural change is about overcoming the present and generating surprising evocations of novelty. Those virtual multiplicities exist with us now (albeit in a highly contracted form), utterly undermining linear conceptions of past, present, and future in the process.

> The virtual is another name for the inherence of the past in the present, for the capacity to become other. As Nietzsche recognized, the weight of the past is also its lightness, its gift. Though we cannot change the past, we can use it to change the present. It is the condition of innovation and the new: the new can only be formed through a kind of eruption or interruption of the present that does not come simply as a gift from the future but is a reworking of the past so that the present is different from itself, is open to eruption. The virtual is the resonance of potential that ladens the present as more than itself, that disrupts the continuity of the present, to open a nick or a crack, the untimely, the unexpected, that welcomes the new, whether a new organism, organ, or function, a new strategy, a new sensation, or a new technical invention. (Grosz 2004: 252)

This is the promise of the Other that is implicit in the writings of Alphonso Lingis and Emmanuel Levinas—a politics of generative difference. What we need is the wherewithal to help them along in their actualization. And this is the utopian function of anthropology, the anthropology of the future. The "capacity to become other" is not the capacity to become *the* other, à la the realization of some already extant possible, but the possibility to overcome the present in an unpredictable, stochastic future defined by brachiating differences.

To say, as critics of utopia often do, that utopia is an oppressive, engineered plan for the future that cannot help but result in dystopia is to miss the point: utopias dredge up—evoke—virtual differences in a negative sense, i.e., they suggest virtualities through their absence. "Thus the 'unknowability thesis' whereby a radically different society cannot even be imagined" evokes new virtualizations through the paucity of their imagining (Jameson 2005: 142).

ANTHROPOLOGY FOR THE FUTURE

In *Histories of the Future* (edited by Daniel Rosenberg and Susan Harding), we can see anthropologists struggling with the effort of freeing the future from its saturnine past, where "our futures feel increasingly citational—each is haunted by the 'semiotic ghosts' of futures past" (Rosenberg and Harding 2004: 4). To visit, as they do, the subdivisions, military bases, and theme parks of the US West is to struggle through the dross of futures past that threaten, indeed, to drag down our own futures under the weight of their (over)representation. To work against the stentorian discourse of progress, they move to the local:

> The grand recits and their characteristic mechanisms (prophecy, prediction, etc.) appear in this book, but always and only in relation to the places, practices, and objects through which they take shape. (Rosenberg and Harding 2005: 14)

But is this enough to escape the gravity well of a future already colonized by the past and present discourses of the neoliberal?

Anna Tsing's contribution looks to the "frontier" in Kalimantan, Indonesia, as both capitulating to capitalist, frontier myth-cycles while at the same time challenging them.

> By this point it should be clear that by "frontier" I do not mean a place or even a process but an imaginative project capable of molding both place and processes. Turner describes the frontier as "the meeting place between savagery and civilization." It is a site of transformation; "the wilderness masters the colonist. . . . Little by little he masters the wilderness." (Tsing 2005: 59)

As she has written many times of globalization in general (cf. Tsing 2000, 2004), however pervasive these discourses may prove, they can only exist in the (local) spaces of their instantiation. And it is in this local practice that possibilities for larger, discursive transformations may be generated: "Frontiers are notoriously unstable, and it is fitting that Kalimantan landscapes should have a role in forging new frontier connections" (2005: 58). Here, those new connections draw together indigenous peoples, settlers, governments, corporations and ecologies in interesting (if potentially ruinous) ways. But there is always the other side, as Tsing reflects on life in Southern California:

> There is truly no there, no directions, no place marks, only faceless serenity, time on hold. Like game in a tree plantation, I felt caught out in the open there, an easy target. Orange County is one kind of nightmare. Its flip side is South Central Los Angeles, the mere thought of which drives masses of whites and Asian Americans behind the Orange Curtain. Time is not on hold in that bastion of short lives. Yet these two nightmares play with each other: just as the fear of hell drives the marketing schemes of paradise, so too does the desire of

paradise fuel the schemes of hell. Both rise and fall on the spectacular performances of savvy entrepreneurs. (Tsing 2005: 55–56)

Whether in Indonesia or Orange County, Hell or Paradise, the "savvy entrepreneurs" ultimately call the shots; i.e., these evocations of Kalimantan futures prove inadequate to the task of reinscribing the future, yet they do, nevertheless, broaden the pool of virtuality. That is, Tsing is not describing some fanciful utopian space where natives continue to live the dreams of a Western imaginary, but a place pierced to the core by global capital. In examining the exploitation of resources in Indonesia, together with the diverse (and unequal) claims of governments, settlers, and indigenes, are there other futures conspicuous, if nothing else, by their absence? Are there other virtualities disclosed in this essay on Kalimantan's actualization? I would argue (perhaps against Tsing herself) that, in the knowledge that Indonesia is not Los Angeles, and in the articulation of this difference, lie potent potentials for alternative actualizations.

Difference has the capacity to stimulate difference. This is the optimistic message in globalization; that its overcoming is inevitable in its diffusion. That is, the oppressive ubiquity of neoliberal regimes is also the engine of their transcendence; as new markets are forced open, as the human genome itself is colonized by capital, so other virtualities multiply that gesture to cultural alterities of a fundamentally unknown future. What Grosz (2004: 152) writes of Nietzsche and Darwin could be just as true of anthropology:

Although Nietzsche has an open hostility to what he perceives is the valuation of the average, of the mediocre and the herd in Darwinism, nevertheless his work is marked by Darwin's own conception of time's positivity. It is post-Darwinism in the sense that it is precisely the Darwinian that must be overcome: the processes that generate the descent of man are also the processes that dictate the end of man and the evolution of the overman. He conceptualizes the future in terms quite consonant with Darwin's understanding of the forward force of time directing life to greater difference, greater variation, greater exploration and experimentation.

We do not look to the future for the legitimation of the present—i.e., the teleological future—but for the future in its capacity to shake our understandings of the past, to remake identity and history. This, more than anything else, is the contribution of anthropology to the future: building the anti-time machine, i.e., not only preventing us from time travel along linear spatialities but in collapsing present, past, and future into a palimpsest of virtualities. Thus: an anthropology for the future rather than of the future.

POSTSCRIPT

In 2018, the Society for Cultural Anthropology published a series of short articles on "Speculative Anthropologies" in their "Fieldsights" section; the contributions are a clear summary of SF-inflected approaches to the future in anthropology, ones that enable "us to confront our world's inclusions and exclusions across imaginaries of difference and thereby challenge the taken-for-granted by pushing boundaries of the individual and society, the human and alien, the planet, and life itself" (Anderson et al. 2018). The question for the short essays in this series: what would such a speculative anthropology mean? For Colon-Cabrera, it is "one that reframes the narrative outside of a colonial framework and removes the white male authority in terms of both theory and practice" (Colon-Cabrera 2018). For Markert and Trombley, a speculative anthropology might have "the power to open up new ways of looking at a complex world; at most, it has the potential to shape it into something better" (Markert and Trombley 2018). Oman-Reagan adds that "speculative ethnography can teach us to imagine justice and freedom as attainable in all our first contacts with today's emerging realities and with the possibly, hopefully more just, futures yet to come" (Oman-Reagan 2018). Here, we can see the power of the speculative in both allowing anthropology to challenge its entrenched inequality while at the same time returning us to the worlds we encounter as anthropologists. And it is here that "speculative anthropology" begins to look like realism—turning away from the ideological blinders of anthropology's time machine in order to see, understand, and communicate the future work of people with whom we study. The science fictions, in other words, were the self-legitimizing, unilinear futures that have heretofore informed the anthropological project.

For me, these short essays represent a remarkable moment in anthropology where anthropology again attends to the future, again invokes the texts and language of science fiction, and, again, wonders what will be—but with a difference. In the 1970s and 1980s, future-work in anthropology remained the servant of capitalism, festooning the linear, developmental scaffolding with the pseudo-flesh of functionalist, cybernetic culture. How would people *adapt* to the new, technological normal? How would that urban, corporate future look and feel? Capitalism, in other words, would always precede us into that future. In contrast, consider the final words of Reese's remarkable ethnography of food apartheid in Washington, DC:

> What does or would it mean for Ms. Johnson to flourish in the ways that she imagines for herself and her community? More specifically, what does it means to flourish in the context of anti-Blackness, displacement, and the constant re-

minders that for the maintenance of the state as it is currently articulated, Black lives have to *not* matter? . . . As we re/imagine our foodscapes near and far, one thing is clear: seeds of good futures that are equitable and sustainable are in the stories, in the hopes, and in the lives of Black residents and organizations that look beyond what they can see and believe in something better. (Reese 2019: 139)

Here, Reese seems to take a page out of Hurston, while at the same time bringing out the revolutionary implications of food justice. What would it mean for anthropologists to document and advocate for futures that represent both a repudiation of current inequalities and oppressions and an acknowledgment that people have already imagined their flourishing? What speculative anthropologies might that involve?

The collection describes a moment of possibility in anthropology, one where the focus might shift toward alternatives and, in so doing, contribute to other "world-makings" alien to the racist, capitalist futures that make up the dross of mass media's impoverished imagination (Kondo 2018). This speculative anthropology might (and should) take many forms, but it needs to start with imagination and empathy. Imagination that other worlds are possible, are worth struggling for, are worth supporting. And empathy for people all over the world who have already conjured up those worlds in their own struggles.

References

Anderson, Reynaldo and Charles E. Jones (2015). "Introduction: The Rise of Astro-Blackness." In *Afrofuturism 2.0: The Rise of Astro-Blackness*. Ed. Reynaldo Anderson and Charles E. Jones, pp. vii–xviii. Lanham, MD: Lexington Books.

Anderson, Ryan (2018). "The Unstable Edge: Anthropology, Speculative Fiction, and the Incremental Threat of Sea Level Rise." Theorizing the Contemporary, Fieldsights, December 18. https://culanth.org/fieldsights/the-unstable-edge-anthropology-speculative-fiction-and-the-incremental-threat-of-sea-level-rise.

Ansell-Pearson, Keith (2002). *Philosophy and the Adventure of the Virtual*. New York: Routledge.

Appadurai, Arjun (1996). *Modernity at Large*. Minneapolis: University of Minnesota Press.

Arnold, Matthew (1882). *Culture and Anarchy*. New York: Macmillan and Co.

Asad, Talal, ed. (1973). *Anthropology and the Colonial Encounter*. New York: Humanities Press.

Ashkenazi, Michael (1995). "Will ETI be Space Explorers?" In *Progress in the Search for Extraterrestrial Life*, ASP Conference Series, vol. 74. Ed. by G. Seth Shostak, pp. 507–515. Bioastronomy Symposium, Santa Cruz, California, August 16–20, 1993.

Augé, Marc (1995). *Non-place*. New York: Verso.

Axel, Brian Keith (2004). "The Context of Diaspora." *American Ethnologist* 19(1): 26–60.

Bandy, Matthew (2004). "Fissioning, Scalar Stress and Social Evolution in Early Village Societies." *American Anthropologist* 106(2): 322–333.

Barber, Benjamin (1996). *Jihad vs. McWorld*. New York: Ballantine Books.

Barnard, Alan (1994). "Tarzan and the Lost Races." In *Exploring the Written*. Ed. Eduardo Archetti, pp. 231–257. Oslo, Norway: Scandinavian University Press.

Barrow, Craig, and Diana Barrow (1991). "Le Guin's Earthsea." *Extrapolation* 32(1): 20–44.

Bartholomew, Robert (1991). "The Quest for Transcendence." *The Anthropology of Consciousness* 2(1–2): 1–12.

Bateson, Gregory (1979). *Mind and Nature*. New York: Dutton.

—— (1979). *Steps to an Ecology of Mind*. New York: Ballantine Books.

Bateson, Gregory and Margaret Mead (1941). "Principles of Morale Building." *Journal of Educational Sociology* 15(4): 206–220.

Bateson, Mary Catherine (1984). *With a Daughter's Eye.* New York: William Morrow and Co.

Battaglia, Deborah, ed. (2005). *E.T. Culture.* Durham, NC: Duke University Press.

Bell, Wendell (1997). *Foundations of Future Studies,* vol. 2. New York: Transaction.

Benedict, Ruth (1934). *Patterns of Culture.* Boston: Houghton Mifflin.

—— (1946). *The Chrysanthemum and the Sword.* Boston: Houghton Mifflin.

Benjamin, Walter (1978). *Reflections.* New York: Schoken Books.

Bennett, Jane (2001). *The Enchantment of Modern Life.* Princeton: Princeton University Press.

Bergson, Henri (1983 [1907]). *Creative Evolution.* Lanham, MD: University Press of America.

Besteman, Catherine, and Hugh Gusterson, eds. (2005). *Why America's Top Pundits are Wrong.* Berkeley: University of California.

Biehl, Joao and Peter Locke, eds (2017). *Unfinished.* Durham, NC: Duke University Press.

Bishop, Michael (1980).*Transfigurations.* New York: Berkeley.

—— (1982). *No Enemy But Time.* New York: Timescape.

Bestor, Theodore C. (2004). *Tsukiji.* Berkeley: University of California.

Boas, Franz (2004 [1932]). *Anthropology of Modern Life.* New Brunswick, NJ: Transaction Publishers.

Bohannan, Paul (1992). *We, the Alien.* Prospect Heights, IL: Waveland Press.

Borofsky, Rob (2005). *Yanomami: the Fierce Controversy.* Berkeley: University of California.

Braude, Ann (2001). *Radical Spirits.* Bloomington, IN: Indiana University Press.

Braun, Werner von (1952). *Das Marsprojekt.* Frankfurt: Umschau Verlag.

Brennan, Timothy (2002). "Cosmo-Theory." The South Atlantic Quarterly 100(3): 659–691.

Brooks, Rodney (1997). "From Earwigs to Autonomous Humans." *Robotics and Autonomous Systems* 20(2–4): 291–304.

Brooks, Rodney, and Anita Flynn (1989). "Fast, Cheap and Out of Control" (AI Memo 1882). Cambridge: MIT Press.

Brumfiel, Elizabeth M., and John W. Fox, eds. (1994). *Factional Competition and Political Development in the New World.* New York: Cambridge University Press.

Bryant, Rebecca and Daniel M. Knight (2019). *The Anthropology of the Future.* NY: Cambridge University Press.

Buck-Morrs, Susan (1989). *The Dialectics of Seeing.* Cambridge: MIT Press.

Butler, Octavia E. (1988 [1979]). *Kindred.* Boston: Beacon Press, 1988.

Caley, Michael (1994). *Mindscapes.* New York: Routledge.

Calhoun, Craig (2002). "Imagining Solidarity." *Public Culture* 14(1): 147–171.

Cantor, Paul, and Peter Hufnagel (2006). "The Empire of the Future." *Studies in the Novel* 38(1): 36–56.

Carneiro, Robert L. (2003). *Evolutionism in Cultural Anthropology.* Boulder, CO: Westview Press.

Cariani, Peter (1991). "Adaptivity and Emergence in Organisms and Devices." *World Futures* 32: 111–132.

Chad Oliver Collection. College Station, TX: Texas A&M Cushing Library.

Chan, Edward K. (2020). "Race in the Bladerunner cycle and demographic dystopia." *Science Fiction Film and Television* 13(1): 59–76.

Chin, Elizabeth and Danya Glabau (2019). "Wakanda University." American Anthropological Annual Meeting, Vancouver, Canada.

Chapdelaine, Perry A., ed. (1987). *The Complete Collection of John W. Campbell Letters.* Franklin, TN: AC Projects. 7 microform reels.

Clark, Andy (2001). *Mindware.* NY: Oxford University Press.

Clark, David L. (2001). "Kant's Aliens: the Anthropology and Its Others." *The New Centennial Review* 1(2): 201–289.

Clark, G. A. (2000). "Darwinian Dystopia." *Futures* 32: 729–738.

Clifford, James (1981). "On Ethnographic Surrealism." *Comparative Studies in Society and History* 23: 539–64.

—— (1986). "Introduction." In *Writing Culture.* Ed. by J. Clifford and G. Marcus, pp. 1–26. Berkeley: University of California Press.

—— (1988). *The Predicament of Culture.* Cambridge: Harvard University Press.

Clfford, James and George R. Marcus (1986). *Writing Culture.* Berkeley: University of California Press.

Clute, John, and Peter Nicholls (1995). *The Encyclopedia of Science Fiction.* New York: St. Martin's Griffin.

Collins, Samuel Gerald (2003). "Sail On! Sail On!" *Science Fiction Studies* 30: 180–198.

—— (2004). "Scientifically Valid and Artistically True." *Science Fiction Studies* 31: 243–263.

—— (2005a). "No Anthropologist Aboard the Enterprise." *Anthropology & Education Quarterly* 36(2): 182–88.

—— (2005b). "Colonies on the Moon/ Cyborgs on the Earth." *International Journal of Humanities* 2(1): 649–657.

—— (2006a). "Imagined Cities, Real Futures." *Reconstruction* 6(1). <reconstruction.eserver.org>. Accessed August, 2007.

—— (2006b). "On Emergent Phenomena." In *An Imitation-Based Approach to Modeling Homogenous Agents Societies.* Ed. by Goran Trajkovski, pp. 93–114. Hershey, PA: IDEA Group.

—— (2007). "Making Magic, Writing Culture." *Social Studies of Science* 37(3): 489–494.

—— (2009). *Library of Walls.* Sacramento, CA: Litwin Books.

—— (2020). "Ethnography Apps and Games." Oxford Bibliographies. https://www.oxfordbibliographies.com/view/document/obo-9780199766567/obo-9780199766567-0230.xml, accessed December 12, 2020.

Collins, Samuel and Goran Trajkovski (2006). "Attack of the Rainbow Robots." In *Diversity in IT Education.* Ed. Goran Trajkovski. Hershey, PA: IDEA Publishing.

Colón-Cabrera, David (2018). "Looking for Humanity in Science Fiction through Afrofuturism." Theorizing the Contemporary, Fieldsights, December 18. https://culanth.org/fieldsights/looking-for-humanity-in-science-fiction-through-afrofuturism.

Cooper, Rachel (2004). "Can Sociologists Understand Other Forms of Life?" *Perspectives on Science* 12(1): 29–54.

Darwin, Charles (1871). *The Descent of Man, and Selection in Relation to Sex.* London: John Murray.

Dassbach, Carl (1993). "Enterprises and B Phases." *Sociological Perspectives* 36(4): 359–375.

Dator, Jim (1998). "Introduction." *American Behavioral Scientist* 42(3): 298–320.

Dean, Jodi (1997). "The Familiarity of Strangeness." *Theory & Event* 1(2).

Deleuze, Gilles (1991). *Bergsonism.* NY: Zone Books.

Deleuze, Gilles, and Félix Guattari (1987). *A Thousand Plateaus.* Minneapolis: University of Minnesota Press.

DeLillo, Don (2003). *Cosmopolis.* New York: Scribner.

Deloria, Vine, Jr. (1969). *Custer Died For Your Sins.* New York: Macmillan.

Desmond, Adrian and James Moore (1991). *Darwin.* London: Penguin.

Diamond, Jared (2005). *Collapse.* New York: Viking.

di Leonardo, Micaela (1998). *Exotics at Home.* Chicago: University of Chicago Press.

Dillon, Wilton S. (1980). "Margaret Mead and Government." *American Anthropologist* 82(2): 318–339.

Earle, Timothy (2004). "Culture Matters in the Neolithic Transition and Emergence of Hierarchy in Thy, Denmark." *American Anthropologist* 106(1): 111–125.

Ehrlich, Paul (1971). *The Population Bomb.* Rivercity, MA: Rivercity Press.

Emmeche, Claus (1994). *The Garden in the Machine.* Princeton: Princeton University Press.

Escobar, Arturo (1995). *Encountering Development.* Princeton: Princeton University Press.

—— (2001). "Reflections on 'Development'." *Futures* (June): 411–435.

—— (2017). *Designs for the Pluriverse.* Durham, NC: Duke University Press.

Eshun, Kodwo (2003). "Further Considerations of Astrofuturism." *New Centennial Review* 3(2): 287–302.

Fabian, Johannes (1983). *Time and the Other.* New York: Columbia University Press.

Ferguson, James (2002). *The Anti-Politics Machine.* Minneapolis: University of Minnesota Press.

Ferrell, Keith (1992). "How to Build an Alien." *Omni* 92 (15.1).

Finney, Ben. (1992). *From Sea to Space.* New Zealand: Massey University Press.

Fischer, Michael M. J. (1999). "Worlding Cyberspace." In *Critical Anthropology Now.* Ed. George Marcus, pp. 245–304. Sante Fe, NM: SAR Press.

—— (2003). *Emergent Forms of Life and the Anthropological Voice.* Durham, NC: Duke.

Fracchia, Joseph and R.C. Lewontin (1999). "Does Culture Evolve?" *History and Theory* 38(4): 52–79.

Frantz, Charles (1966). "Review of *Continuities in Cultural Evolution*." *Current Anthropology* 7(1): 70–71.

Frazer, James George (1922). *The Golden Bough.* New York: McMillan and Co.

Fukuyama, Francis (1992). *The End of History and the Last Man.* New York: Penguin.

Funaro, Jim (1994). "The Evolution of COTI." <www.contact-conference.com>. Accessed June, 2005.

Garber, S. J. (1999). "Searching for Good Science." *Journal of the British Interplanetary Society* 52: 3–12.

Gell, Alfred (1992). *The Anthropology of Time.* Providence, RI: Berg.

Gibson, William (1989). Interview (February) with Terry Gross on "Fresh Air." Washington, DC: National Public Radio.

—— (2001). "My Own Private Tokyo." *Wired* 9.09.

Gilder, George (2006). "The Information Factory." *Wired* 14.10.

Gill, Lelsey (2004). *School of the Americas.* Durham, NC: Duke University Press.

Ginsburg, Faye, and Fred Myers (2006). "A History of Aboriginal Futures." *Critique of Anthropology* 26(1): 27–45.

Goldschmidt, Walter (1959). *Man's Way.* New York: Holt, Rinehart and Winston.

Gorer, Geoffrey (1943). "Japanese Character Structure." *Transactions of the New York Academy of Sciences,* Series II, 5(5): 106–124.

Gorman, Alice (2019). *Dr Space Junk vs The Universe.* Cambridge, MA: The MIT Press.

Gould, Stephen Jay (1981). *The Mismeasure of Man.* New York: W.W. Norton.

—— (2002). *The Structure of Evolutionary Theory.* Cambridge, MA: Harvard University Press.

Graeber, David (2014). "What's the Point If We Can't Have Fun?" *The Baffler* 24: 50–58.

Gregg, Dorothy, and Elgin Williams (1948). "The Dismal Science of Functionalism." *American Anthropologist* 50: 594–611.

Grosz, Elizabeth (1999). "Thinking of the New." In *Becomings.* Ed. Grosz. Ithaca, NY: Cornell University Press.

—— (2004). *The Nick of Time.* Durham, NC: Duke University Press.

Hakken, David, and Barbara Andrews (1993). *Computing Myths and Class Realities.* Boulder, CO: Westview Press.

Hale, Charles (2006). "Activist Research v. Cultural Critique." *Cultural Anthropology* 21(1): 96–120.

Hall, Hal W. (1989). *The Work of Chad Oliver.* San Bernadino, CA: The Borgo Press.

Haller, John S., Jr. (1971). "Race and the Concept of Progress in Nineteenth Century American Ethnology." *American Anthropologist* 73(3): 710–24.

Handler, Richard (1990). "Boasian Anthropology and the Critique of American Culture." *American Quarterly* 42(2): 252–273.

——, ed. (2000). *Excluded Ancestors, Inventible Traditions: History of Anthropology,* v. 9. Madison: University of Wisconsin Press.

Hannerz, Ulf (2003). "Macro-scenarios." *Social Anthropology* 11: 169–187.

Haraway, Donna (2016). *Staying With the Trouble.* Durham, NC: Duke University Press.

Harkins, Arthur, and Margoroh Maruyama (1973). "Rules for Anthropologists: The Future Is Now." *CAE Newsletter* 4(2): 27–32.

Harris, Lee (2004). *Civilization and Its Enemies.* New York: Free Press.

Harrison, Ira E., and Faye V. Harrison, eds. (1999). *African American Pioneers of Anthropology.* Urbana: University of Illinois Press.

Harris, Marvin (1974). *Cows, Pigs, Wars, and Witches.* New York: Random House.

Harvey, David (1989). *The Condition of Postmodernity.* Cambridge: Basil Blackwell.

—— (2000). *Spaces of Hope.* Berkeley: University of California Press.

Haydu, George G. (1966). "Review of *Continuities in Cultural Evolution.*" *Current Anthropology* 7(1): 73–74.

Hayles, N. Katherine (1999). *How We Became Post-Human.* Chicago: University of Chicago Press.

Heinlein, Robert A. (1957) "All You Zombies." *Fantasy and Science Fiction* (March).

Helmreich, Stefan (1998). *Silicon Second Nature.* Berkeley: University of California Press.

—— (2001). "Trees and Seas of Information." *American Ethnologist* 30(3): 340–358.

Hendry, Joy (2003). "An Ethnographer in the Global Arena." *Global Networks* 3(4): 497–512.

Herzfeld, Michael (2001). *Anthropology.* New York: Blackwell Publishers.

Hess, John, and Karen Hess (2000). *The Taste of America.* Champagne-Urbana, Ill.: University of Illinois Press.

Hollinger, Veronica (2006). "Stories About the Future." *Science Fiction Studies* 33(3).

Hope, Cristal (2003). "Futurism is Dead." *Wired* 11.2.

Horowitz, David (2006). *The Professors.* Washington, D.C.: Regnery Publishing, Inc.

Howard, Jane (1984). *Margaret Mead.* New York: Fawcett Columbine.

Huntington, Samuel (1993). "The Clash of Civilizations?" *Foreign Affairs* 72(3): 22–49.

Hyatt, M. (1990). *Franz Boas, Social Activist.* Westport, CT: Greenwood Press.

Hymes, Dell, ed. (1972). *Reinventing Anthropology.* New York: Random House.

Jameson, Fredric (1975). "World-Reduction in Le Guin." *Science Fiction Studies* 2: 3.

—— (2005). *Archaeologies of the Future.* New York: Verso.

Jennings, Michael (2003). "On the Banks of a New Lethe." *Boundary 2* 30(1): 89–104.

Johnson, J. C., and Ben Finney (1986). "Structural Approach to the Study of Groups in Space." *Journal of Social Behavior and Personality* 1(3): 325–347.

Johnston, John (2002). "A Future for Autonomous Agents." *Configurations* 10(3): 473–516.

Jones, Eric M. and Ben R. Finney (1985). "Fastships and Nomads." In *Interstellar Migration and the Human Experience.* Ed. Jones and Finney, pp. 88–104. Berkeley: University of California Press.

Kadir, Nazima (2006). "Class War at Yale." *Anthropology News* 47(8): 12–13.

Kahn, Herman (1961). *On Thermonuclear War.* Princeton: Princeton University Press.

Kahn, Herman, William Brown, and Leon Martel (1976). *The Next 200 Years.* New York: Morrow.

Kaplan, Martha (1995). *Neither Cargo Nor Cult.* Durham, NC: Duke University Press.

Kapoor, Rakeesh, ed. (2004). *Indian Futures: Special Issue of Futures* 36:6/7.

Kelly, Patricia (2002). "Occupied Territory." *Futures* 34: 561–570.

Ketterer, David (1974). *New Worlds for Old.* Bloomington, IN: Indiana University Press.

Keur, Dorothy and Russell La Due (1978). "Univaria." In *Cultures of the Future.* Ed. by Margoroh Maruyama and Arthur Harkins, pp. 593–612. Chicago: Mouton.

Kiernan, Egan (2002). *Getting It Wrong from the Beginning.* New Haven, CT: Yale University Press.

Kilgore, D. W. (2003). *Astrofuturism.* Philadelphia: University of Pennsylvania Press.

Klass, Morton (1989). "Earthman's Burden." In *The Crash of Empires.* Ed. J. Pournelle and J. F. Carr, pp. 206–218. New York: Baen Publishing Enterprises.

Klerkx, Greg (2004). *Lost in Space: The Fall of NASA and the Dream of a New Space Age.* New York: Pantheon Books.

Knowles, Thomas W. (1990). "Chad Oliver Interview #1 Transcript." Unpublished transcript eventually published as "Returning to his First Love," *Bryan-College Station Eagle,* 1C+ (2/25/90).

Kondo, Dorinne (2018). *World-Making.* Durham, NC: Duke University Press.

Kottak, Conrad Phillip (2004). "An Anthropological Take on Sustainable Development." *Human Organization* 63(4): 501–510.

Kottler, Malcolm Jay (1974). "Alfred Russel Wallace, the Origin of Man, and Spiritualism." *Isis* 65(2): 144–192.

Kurasawa, Fuyuki (2004). *The Ethnological Imagination.* Minneapolis, MN: University of Minnesota Press.

Kurzweil, Ray (2006). *The Singularity is Near.* New York: Penguin.

Lakoff, George (2004). *Don't Think of an Elephant.* New York: Chelsea Green Publishing Co.

Latour, Bruno (1993). *We Have Never Been Modern.* Cambridge: Harvard University Press.

Lavender, Isiah (2016). "An Astrofuturist Reading of Zora Neale Hurston's Their Eyes Were Watching God." *LIT* 27(3): 213–233.

Lefferts, H.L. (1978). "The State of Anthropology Today." In *Cultures of the Future.* Ed. Margoroh Maruyama and Arthur Harkins, pp. 692–731. Chicago: Mouton.

Le Guin, Ursula K. (1989). "Is Gender Necessary? Redux." *The Language of the Night.* Ed. Susan Wood, pp. 155–172. New York: HarperCollins.

Lempert, Robert, Steve Popper, and Steven Bankes (2003). *Shaping the Next One Hundred Years.* Washington, DC: RAND Corporation.

Lempert, William (2018). "Planeterra Nullius: Science Fiction Writing and the Ethnographic Imagination." Theorizing the Contemporary, Fieldsights, December 18. https://culanth.org/fieldsights/planeterra-nullius-science-fiction-writing-and-the-ethnographic-imagination.

Lepselter, Susan (2005). "Why Rachel Isn't Buried at Her Grave." In *Histories of the Future.* Ed. D. Rosenberg and S. Hardings, pp. 255–280. Durham, NC: Duke University Press.

Letwin, Shirley (1982). "Matthew Arnold: Enemy of Tradition." *Political Theory* 10(3): 333–351.

Lewin, Roger (1999). *Complexity: Life at the Edge of Chaos.* Chicago: University of Chicago Press.

LiPuma, Edward and Benjamin Lee (2004). *Financial Derivatives and the Globalization of Risk.* Durham, NC: Duke University Press.

Margaret Mead papers and South Pacific Ethnographic Archives, 1838–1996. Washington, D.C. Library of Congress Manuscript Division.

Marien, Michael (2006). "Tofflerana, New and (Mostly) Old." *The Futurist* 11: 62–63.

Marin, Louis (1993). "Frontiers of Utopia." *Critical Inquiry* 19(3): 397–420.

Marcus, George and Michael M.J. Fischer (1986). *Anthropology as Cultural Critique.* Chicago: University of Chicago Press.

Markert, Patricia, and Jeremy Trombley (2018). "Fieldnotes from the Twilight Zone." Theorizing the Contemporary, Fieldsights, December 18. https://culanth.org/fieldsights/fieldnotes-from-the-twilight-zone.

Martin, Emily (1994). *Flexible Bodies.* Boston: Beacon Press.

Maruyama, Magoroh and Arthur Harkins, eds. (1975). *Cultures Beyond the Earth.* New York: Vintage.

Matheson, Richard (1997[1954]). *I Am Legend.* NY: Orb Books.

McCallum, Cecilia (2005). "Racialized Bodies, Naturalized Classes: Moving through the city of Salvador da Bahia." *American Ethnologist* 32(1): 100–117.

McConnell, B. (2001). *Beyond Contact.* Sebastopol, CA: O'Reilly.

Mead, Margaret (1942). *And Keep Your Powder Dry.* New York: Morrow.

—— (1943). "The Problem of Changing Food Habits." *Bulletin of the Menninger Foundation* VII(2).

—— (1955). *Soviet Attitudes Towards Authority.* New York: Tavistock Publications.

—— (1956). *New Lives for Old.* New York: Morrow.

—— (1957). "Towards More Vivid Utopias." *Science* 126(3280): 957–61.

—— (1959). "Apprenticeship Under Boas." In *The Anthropology of Franz Boas.* Ed. Walter Goldschmidt. Memoir No. 89 of the American Anthropological Association. Washington, DC: American Anthropological Association.

—— (1964). *Continuities in Cultural Evolution.* New Haven, CT: Yale University Press.

—— (1966). "Author's Précis." *Current Anthropology* 7(1): 67–68.

—— (1970). *Culture and Commitment.* NY: Doubleday.

—— (1972). *Blackberry Winter.* New York: Morrow.

—— (2005). *The World Ahead.* Ed. Robert B. Textor. NY: Berghahn Books.

Meadows, Donella, Jorgen Randes, and Dennis Meadows (2004). *Limits to Growth.* Whire River Junction, VT: Chelsea Green Publishing.

Messeri, Lisa (2016). *Placing Outer Space.* Durham, NC: Duke University Press.

Meyer, Birgit and Peter Pels, eds. (2003). *Magic and Modernity.* Stanford: Stanford University Press.

Miéville, China (1998). "China Miéville on World Building." *Del Rey Internet Newsletter* 97. www.randomhouse.com/delrey.

—— (2001a). *Perdido Street Station.* New York: Del Rey.

—— (2001b). "Author Spotlight: China Mieville." www.randomhouse.com.

—— (2018). "A Strategy for Ruination." Boston Review. https://bostonreview.net/literature-culture-china-mieville-strategy-ruination, accessed November 6, 2020.

Mignolo, Walter D. (2000). "The Many Faces of Cosmo-polis." *Public Culture* 12(3): 721–748.

Miyazaki, Hirokazu (2004). *The Method of Hope.* Stanford, CA: Stanford University Press.

Moldrup, C., J.M. Morgall, and A.B. Almarsdottir (2002). "Perceived Risk of Future Drugs." *Health, Risk and Society* 4(1): 5–14.

Montagu, Ashley (1973). In *Life Beyond Earth & the Mind of Man.* Ed. R. Berendzen, pp. 21–28. Washington, D.C.: NASA.

Moskowitz, B. (1975). "The Moral Obligations of Anthropology." In *Cultures Beyond the Earth.* Ed. M. Maruyama and A. Harkins, pp. 64–82. New York: Vintage Books, 1975.

Mueller, Karl, et al. (2006). *Striking First.* Washington, D.C.: RAND Corporation.

Mullins, David (2006). "Exploring Change in the Housing Association Sector Using the Delphi Method." *Housing Studies* 21(2): 227–251.

Munn, Nancy D. (1992). "The Cultural Anthropology of Time." *Annual Review of Anthropology* 21: 93–123.

Murphy, Robin R.(2000). *Introduction to AI Robotics.* Cambridge: MIT Press.

Naisbitt, John (1988). *Megatrends.* NY: Grand Central Publishing.

NASA (1999). *Workshop on the Societal Implications of Astrobiology: Final Report.* NASA Technical Memorandum, Ames Research Center.

Nazarea, Virginia D. (1998). *Cultural Memory and Biodiversity.* Tuscon: University of Arizona Press.

Nelson, Diane (2001). "Phantom Limbs." *Cultural Anthropology* 16(3): 303–313.

Oliver, Chad (1948). "The Imperfect Machine." *Texas Literary Quarterly* 1(1): 21–25.

—— (1952). "The Builded a Tower." Unpublished MA Thesis. University of Texas.

—— (1953). "Technical Advisor." *The Magazine of Fantasy and Science Fiction* 4: 30–40.

—— (1954). *Shadows in the Sun.* New York: Ballantine Books.

—— (1955a). "Mother of Necessity." In *Another Kind.* Pp. 1–14. New York: Ballantine Books.

—— (1955b). "Night." In *Another Kind.* Pp. 74–96. New York: Ballantine Books.

—— (1957). *The Winds of Time.* Garden City, NY: Doubleday.

—— (1962). *Ecology and Cultural Continuity as Contributing Factors in the Social Organization of the Plains Indians.* Berkeley: University of California Press.

—— (1965a). "The End of the Line." *The Magazine of Fantasy and Science Fiction* 28: 5–31.

—— (1965b). "A Stick for Harry Eddington." *The Magazine of Fantasy and Science Fiction* 29 (Aug.): 81–95.

—— (1965c). "Individuality, Freedom of Choice, and Cultural Flexibility of the Kamba." *American Anthropologist* 67(2): 421–428.

—— (1967). *The Wolf is My Brother.* New York: Signet Books.

—— (1971 [1953]). "The Ant and the Eye." In *The Edge of Forever.* Pp. 177–228. Los Angeles: Sherbourne Press.

—— (1971 [1954]). "Field Expedient." In *The Edge of Forever.* Pp. 122–176. Los Angeles: Sherbourne Press.

—— (1972). "King of the Hill." *Again, Dangerous Visions.* Ed. Harlan Ellison, pp. 170–186. Garden City, NY: Doubleday.

—— (1974a). "Two Horizons of Man." Unpublished AAA Paper.

—— (1974b [1970]). "Far From This Earth." In *Anthropology Through Science Fiction.* Ed. Carol Mason, Martin Harry Greenberg ,and Patricia S. Warrick, pp. 201–215. New York: St. Martin's Press.

—— (1974c). "The Gift." In *Future Kin.* Ed. Roger Elwood, pp. 33–60. Garden City, NY: Doubleday.

—— (1981). *The Discovery of Humanity.* New York: Harper and Row.

—— (1982). "The Hills and the Plains." In *Culture and Ecology.* Ed. John G. Kennedy and Robert B. Edgerton, pp. 142–157. Washington, DC: American Anthropological Association.

—— (1983). "Ghost Town." *Analog* (September): 11–27.

—— (1984a). *Unearthly Neighbors.* New York: Crown Publishers.

—— (1984b [1971]). *The Shores of Another Sea.* New York: Crown Publishers.

—— (1984c). "Afterword." In *The Shores of Another Sea.* New York: Crown Publishers.

—— (1989). *Broken Eagle.* NY: Bantam Books.

—— (1994). *Cannibal Owl.* NY: Domain Press.

—— (2003 [1951]). "The Edge of Forever." In *A Star Above It.* Ed. P. Olson, pp. 165–186. Framingham, MA: The NESFA Press.

Olson, Valerie (2018). *Into the Extreme.* Minneapolis, MN: University of Minnesota Press.

O'Neill, Gerard (1976). *The High Frontier.* New York: Morrow.

Oman-Reagan, Michael (2018). "First Contact with Possible Futures." Theorizing the Contemporary, Fieldsights, December 18. https://culanth.org/fieldsights/first-contact-with-possible-futures.

Ong, Aihwa (2002). *Buddha is Hiding.* Berkeley: University of California Press.

Oppenheim, Janet (1985). *The other world.* NY: Cambridge University Press.

Palinkas, L. (1990). "Psychosocial effects of adjustment in Antarctica: Lessons for long-duration space flight." *Journal of Spacecraft and Rockets* 27: 471–77.

Palumbo-Liu, David (2002). "Multiculturalism Now." *Boundary 2* 29(2): 109–127.

Pandian, Anand (2019). *A Possible Anthropology.* Durham, NC: Duke University Press.

Pels, Peter (1999). "Professions of Duplexity." *Current Anthropology* 40(2): 101–136.

—— (2003). "Spirits of Modernity." In *Magic and Modernity.* Ed. B. Meyer and P. Pels, pp. 241–271. Stanford: Stanford University Press.

Peterson, John (1984). "Our Past, Chad Oliver's Future." *The Austin Chronicle* (21 December 1984) 4: 9.

Pickering, Andrew (1995). *The Mangle of Practice.* Chicago: University of Chicago Press.

Pierpoint, Claudia Roth (2004). "The Measure of America." *The New Yorker* (8 March): 48–63.

Popem, Shari (2002). "Democratic Pedagogy and the Discourse of Containment." *Anthropology and Education Quarterly* 33(3): 383–394.

Price, David (1998). "Gregory Bateson and the OSS." *Human Organization* 57(4): 379–384.

—— (2004). *Threatening Anthropology.* Durham, NC: Duke University Press.

Rabinow, Paul (1999). *French DNA.* Chicago: University of Chicago Press.

Radin, Paul (1987 [1933]). *Method and Theory of Ethnology.* South Hadley, MA: Bergin & Garvey.

Rapp, Rayna (1999). *Testing Women, Testing the Fetus.* New York: Routledge.

Rauch, Jonathan (2002). "Seeing Around Corners." *Atlantic Monthly* 289(4): 35–47.

Razak, Victoria (1996). "From the Canvas to the Field." *Futures* 28(6–7): 645–649.

Razak, Victoria, and Sam Cole (1995). "Anthropological Perspectives on the Future of Culture and Society." *Futures* 27(4): 375–384.

Reese, Ashante (2019). *Black Food Geographies*. Chapel Hill, NC: University of North Carolina Press.

Rejeski, David, and Robert L. Olson (2006). "Has Futurism Failed?" *Wilson Quarterly* 30(1): 14–21.

Riner, Reed (1982). "Editorial." *Cultural Futures Research* 7(1): 3.

—— (1987). "Doing Futures Research—Anthropologically." *Futures* 19(3): 311–328.

—— (1991). "Anthropology About the Future—Limits and Potentials." *Human Organization* 50(3): 297–311.

—— (1998). "The Future as a Sociocultural Problem." *American Behavioral Scientist* 42(3): 347–364.

—— (2000). "The Contact Hypothesis." In *When SETI Succeeds*. Ed. Allen Tough, pp. 127–138. Bellevue, WA: Foundation for the Future.

Riner, Reed, and Jennifer Clodius (1995). "Simulating Future Histories." *Anthropology of Education Quarterly* 26(1): 95–104.

Ritzer, George (2000). *The McDonaldization of Society*. Boston: Pine Forge Press.

Ronald, Edmund M.A., and Moshe Sipper (2001). "Surprise Versus Unsurprise." *Robotics and Autonomous Systems* 37: 19–24.

Ronald, Edmund M.A., Moshe Sipper and Mathieu S. Capcarrère (1999). "Design, Observation, Surprise!" *Artificial Life* 5(3): 225–239.

Rosenberg, Daniel and Susan Harding, eds. (2005). *Histories of the Future*. Durham: Duke University Press.

—— (2005). "Introduction: Histories of the Future." In *Histories of the Future*. Ed. Daniel Rosenberg and Susan Harding, pp. 1–18. Durham: Duke University Press.

Ross, Andrew (2004). *No Collar: The Humane Workplace and Its Hidden Costs*. Philadelphia: Temple University Press.

Roth, Christopher (2005). "Ufology as Anthropology." In *E.T. Culture*. Ed. by Deborah Battaglia, pp. 38–93. Durham: Duke University Press.

Rothstein, Edward (2003). "Utopia and Its Discontents." In *Visions of Utopia*. Ed. Edward Rothstein, Herbert Muschamp, and Martin E. Marty, pp. 1–28. NY: Oxford University Press.

Rowell, Charles H. (1997). "An Interview With Octavia E. Butler." *Callaloo* 20(1): 47–66.

Russell, M. D. (1996). *The Sparrow*. New York: Ballantine Books.

Sabia, Daniel (2002). "Utopia as Critique." *Peace Review* 14(2): 191–197.

Sahlins, Marshall (1960). "Evolution: Specific and General." In *Evolution and Culture*. Ed. Marshall Sahlins and Elman Service, pp. 12–44. Ann Arbor: University of Michigan Press.

Sahn, Seung (1997). *The Compass of Zen*. Boston: Shambala.

Said, Edward (2001). "The Clash of Ignorance." *The Nation* 273(12): 11–13.

Salazar, Juan, Sarah Pink, Andrew Irving and Johannes Sjoberg, eds (2017). *Anthropologies and Futures*. NY: Bloomsbury

Sawyer, Keith (2001). "Emergence in Sociology." *American Journal of Sociology* 107(3): 551–586.

—— (2002). "Durkheim's Dilemma: Toward a Sociology of Emergence." *Sociological Theory* 20(2): 227–247.

Sennett, Richard (1990). *The Conscience of the Eye*. New York: Faber and Faber.

Shannon, Christopher (1995). "A World Made Safe for Differences." *American Quarterly* 47(4): 659–680.

Sippanondha, Ketudat (1990). *The Middle Path for the Future of Thailand*. Honolulu: East-West Center.

Slotten, Ross A. (2004). *The Heretic in Darwin's Court*. New York: Columbia University Press.

Steward, Julian (1953). "Evolution and Process." *Anthropology Today*. Ed. Alfred Kroeber, pp. 313–326. Chicago: University of Chicago Press.

Stocking, George (1987). *Victorian Anthropology*. New York: Free Press.

—— (1992). *The Ethnographer's Magic and Other Essays in the History of Anthropology*. Madison: University of Wisconsin Press.

Stone, M. Priscilla (2003). "Is Sustainability for Development Anthropologists?" *Human Organization* 62(2): 93–99.

Strathern, Marilyn (1992). *Reproducing the Future*. New York: Routledge.

—— (2002). "Emergent Relations." In *Scientific Authorship*. Ed. Mario Biagioli and Peter Galison, pp. 165–194. New York: Routledge.

Styers, Randall (2004). *Making Magic*. New York: Oxford.

Szeman, Imre, and Maria Whiteman (2004). "Future Politics." *Science Fiction Studies* 31(2).

Tatsuya Morita et al. (2005). "Development of a Clinical Guideline for Palliative Sedation Therapy Using the Delphi Method." *Journal of Palliative Medicine* 8(4): 716–729.

Terranova, Tiziana (2004). *Network Culture*. Ann Arbor, MI: Pluto Press.

Textor, Robert (1995a). "Why Anticipatory Anthropology?" *General Anthropology* 6(1): 1–2.

—— (1995b). "The Ethnographic Futures Research Method." *Futures* 27(4): 461–471.

—— (2003). "Honoring Excellence in Anticipatory Anthropology." *Futures* 35(5): 521–527.

—— (2005). "Editor's Commentary." In *The World Ahead*. Ed. Textor. New York: Berghahn Books.

Toffler, Alvin, ed. (1972). *The Futurists*. New York: Random House.

Traweek, Sharon (1988). *Beamtimes and Lifetimes*. Cambridge, MA: Harvard University Press.

Trigger, Bruce (1998). *Sociocultural Evolution*. Malden, MA.: Blackwell Publishers.

Trouillot, Michel-Rolph (1991). "Anthropology and the Savage Slot." *Recapturing Anthropology*. Ed. Richard Fox, pp. 17–44. Sante Fe, NM: SAR Press.

Tsing, Anna (2000). "The Global Situation." *Cultural Anthropology* 15(3): 327–360.

—— (2004). *Friction.* Princeton, NJ: Princeton University Press.

—— (2005). "How to Make Resources in Order to Destroy Them (and Then Save Them?) on the Salvage Frontier." In *Histories of the Future.* Ed. Daniel Rosenberg and Susan Harding, pp. 51–74. Durham, NC: Duke University Press.

Tuastad, Dag (2003). "Neo-Orientalism and the New Barbarian Thesis." *Third World Quarterly* 24(4): 591–599.

Tylor, Edward B. (1958 [1871, 1873]). *The Origins of Culture and Religion in Primitive Culture.* Volumes I and II of the 1871 edition. New York: Harper and Brothers.

Tylor, Stephen (1986). *The Unspeakable.* Madison: University of Wisconsin Press.

US Congress (1961). "Proposed Studies on the Implications of Peaceful Space Activities for Human Affairs." Report of the Committee on Science and Astronautics, US House of Representatives, Eighty-Seventh Congress. Prepared for NASA by the Brookings Institution. Washington, DC: GPO.

Valentine, David and Amelia Hassoun (2019). "Uncommon Futures." *Annual Review of Anthropology* 48: 243–260.

Varela, Francisco (1999). *Ethical Know-How.* Stanford: Stanford University Press.

Varela, Francisco, Evan Thompson, and Eleanor Rosch (1991). *The Embodied Mind.* Cambridge, MA: MIT Press.

Vickers, Brian (1992). "Francis Bacon and the Progress of Knowledge." *Journal of the History of Ideas* 53(3): 495–518.

Virilio, Paul (1986 [1977]). *Speed and Politics.* New York: Semiotext(e).

Wagar, W. Warren (1999). *A Short History of the Future.* Chicago: University of Chicago Press.

Wallace, Alfred Russel (1864). "The Origins of Human Races Deduced From the Theory of Natural Selection." *Journal of the Anthropological Society of London, v. 2*: clviii–clxxxvii.

Wallerstein, Immanuel (2000). "Globalization or the Age of Transition." *International Sociology* 15(2): 251–267.

Wallman, Sandra (1992). *Contemporary Futures.* New York: Routledge.

Wargames (1983). Directed by John Badham. MGM.

Waterston, Alisse, and Maria D. Vesperi. "The Ethnographer's Tale." *Anthropology Newsletter* (March, 2003): 12.

Wells, H. G. (1905). *A Modern Utopia.* London: Chapman and Hall.

—— (1979[1895]). "The Time Machine." In *The Complete Science Fiction Treasury,* pp. 3–68. New York: Crown Publishers.

Werth, L. F. (1998). The Anthropocentric Predicament and the Search for Extraterrestrial Intelligence. *Journal of Applied Philosophy* 15(1): 83–88.

Weston, Kath (2002). *Gender in Real Time.* New York: Routledge.

Westwood, Sally (2000). "Re-branding Britain." *Sociology* 34: 185–202.

White, Donna R. (1999). *Dancing With Dragons.* Columbia, SC: Camden House.

Wired (2006). "Six Trends that are Changing the World." *Wired* 14.07 (July).

Wiener, Norbert (1961). *Cybernetics.* Cambridge: the MIT Press.

Williams, Sarah (1995). "'Perhaps Images at One with the World are Already Lost Forever'." In *The Cyborg Handbook.* Ed. by Chris Hables Gray, pp. 379–392. New York: Routledge.

Wolf, Eric (1982). *Europe and the People Without History*. Berkeley: University of California Press.

Wolf-Meyer, Matthew (2020). *Theory of the World to Come*. Minneapolis, MN: University of Minnesota Press.

Womack, Ytasha (2013). *Afrofuturism*. Chicago: Lawrence Hill Books.

Woolridge, Michael (2002). *An Introduction to Multiagent Systems*. New York: Wiley.

Index